THIS OUTSIDE LIFE

LAURIE KEHLER

HARVEST HOUSE PUBLISHERS
EUGENE, OREGON

Cover by Brian Bobel Design

Cover photo © Aleksandar Novoselski / Stocksy

Published in association with the literary agency of D.C. Jacobson & Associates LLC, an Author Management Company. www.dcjacobson.com

This Outside Life
Published by Harvest House Publishers
Eugene, Oregon 97408
www.harvesthousepublishers.com

ISBN 978-0-7369-7579-7 (pbk.)
ISBN 978-0-7369-7580-3 (eBook)

Library of Congress Cataloging-in-Publication Data

Names: Kehler, Laurie Ostby, author.
Title: This outside life / Laurie Ostby Kehler.
Description: Eugene : Harvest House Publishers, 2018.
Identifiers: LCCN 2018034453 (print) | LCCN 2018039569 (ebook) | ISBN 9780736975803 (ebook) | ISBN 9780736975797 (pbk.)
Subjects: LCSH: Nature--Religious aspects--Christianity--Meditations. | Creation--Meditations. | Spirituality--Christianity.
Classification: LCC BS660 (ebook) | LCC BS660 .K44 2018 (print) | DDC 231.7--dc23
LC record available at https://lccn.loc.gov/2018034453

Printed in the United States of America

19 20 21 22 23 24 25 26 27 / BP-GL / 10 9 8 7 6 5 4 3 2 1

Contents

For Tom and Jack—
I love adventuring with you guys!

For more resources related to this book, visit:
www.ThisOutsideLife.com/bookresources

Why Nature Matters

I've been riveted, hidden in a nature blind with my grandmother watching peregrine falcons hurtle down from the heavens at over 200 miles an hour. I've been delighted at neon pink and purple sea slugs 80 feet underwater. I've been charmed watching cardinals feed each other berries. I've been thrilled witnessing falling stars. I've been surprised by seals joining me while paddleboarding. I've been thunderstruck at the immensity and power of downpours in an Australian rain forest. I'm constantly amazed and delighted by all that goes on in this gorgeous world made by God.

And I believe God wants us to notice it all.

You don't have to go white-water rafting, scuba diving, backpacking, or traveling to distant countries. You can step outside your backdoor. Just sitting there every morning with your cup of coffee for five minutes will enlighten you tremendously. You will begin to notice things. What birds are hanging around? What did the frost do to the daffodils beginning to emerge? Are there any gophers digging up the lawn? What flowers do the snails prefer to eat? What direction does the wind usually come from? And many other nuances of nature. Just step outside, notice, and delight in the "good" that God is doing.

I'm constantly amazed and delighted by all that goes
on in this gorgeous world made by God.

In the beginning, while He made the world, repeatedly we read the phrase, "And God saw that it was good" (Genesis 1). After each step, He is pleased and calls it "good." I imagine, in a small way, it's like when we do something well. You nailed that birthday party. You figured out how to fix something. You created a meal or a painting, and it turned out well. You know it, and you are pleased. Although with Him, it is not only "good." It is perfect and beautiful.

The world He has made is His first revelation of Himself, of His character, and of His design sense, and is a reflection of what He delights in. "For since the creation of the world God's invisible qualities—his eternal power and divine nature—have been clearly seen, being understood from what has been made, so that people are without excuse" (Romans 1:20). God's divine nature is clearly seen through the beauty, wonder, and science of what He has made. And we do well to ponder it. David writes, "When I consider your heavens, the work of your fingers, the moon and the stars, which you have set in place, what is mankind that you are mindful of them, human beings that you care for them?" (Psalm 8:3-4).

God's handiwork is not only beautiful, it's healthful. It is good *for* us. Good for us to live in, eat from, and delight in. In Florence Williams's fascinating book *The Nature Fix*, she describes what walking in nature does for our bodies and minds. According to the latest findings in science, just walking in nature for around 30-45 minutes alone (preferably in evergreen woods and/or near running water or the ocean) has a similar effect on our systems as a daily antidepressant pill. Also, being in nature elevates our NK (natural killer) cells to ward off disease.

God's divine nature is clearly seen through the beauty,
wonder, and science of what He has made.
And we do well to ponder it.

Japan and South Korea are so convinced about the biological benefits of being in nature that they are dedicating more and more acreage and parks to the practice of "Forest Bathing" or *Shinrin Yoku*.
In this experience, you walk along, paying particular attention to
the sights and smells around you. You break branches to smell the
sharp tang of the cypress oils. You breathe deeply and close your eyes.
You get present. You unwind. This is Forest Bathing, and although
it sounds woo-woo, the science is impressive. And who among us
doesn't feel better after a walk outside? But unfortunately, the most
outside many of us get is scurrying from our car to the office or home.
And for our children, it's even more important that they get outside.

Kids need nature. James Sallis says, "Based on previous studies,
we can definitely say that the best predictor of preschool children's
physical activity is simply being outdoors, and that an indoor, seden-
tary childhood is linked to mental-health problems."[1] Another study
on the effect of nature and children came to these conclusions:

> Access to green space was associated with improved men-
> tal well-being, overall health and cognitive development
> of children. It promotes attention restoration, mem-
> ory, competence, supportive social groups, self-discipline,
> moderates stress, improves behaviors and symptoms of
> ADHD and was even associated with higher standardized
> test scores.[2]

Finnish students don't start school until age seven and spend a
large amount of time outdoors even after they begin formal school-
ing. (Fifteen minutes every hour.) Yet they consistently score higher

than most other children in the world and have superior literacy skills. Who wouldn't want all those benefits for their kids?

But we are afraid. We don't want to let our kids roam around outside unattended. So go with them. Find a forest, find a park, go with friends where they can roam and play without having to be on an organized team or a play structure. Find a puddle to look for insects and tadpoles. Have them sniff evergreen branches. Encourage your child to get messy, dirty, and inquisitive. One of my proudest moments at the park was when I was the only mother who would let her child play in a mud puddle.

I remember one rainy spring afternoon I had had it. I was lonely, and my toddler was stir-crazy. I was sick of being cooped up inside day after day due to the rain. "All right," I said, "Let's pretend we live in the Pacific Northwest. They don't stay inside because of rain, and neither will we." I got him dressed in rain boots and raincoat, and I dressed the same. We went outside and started hunting for frogs. We lifted up flowerpots and chairs and unraveled the hose and found several hidden within the folds. He squealed with delight. We stomped in puddles and tried to make the biggest splashes possible. We lifted up stones and hunted for plump earthworms.

There was a small creek, more like a rivulet in a ditch across the road. I made simple foil "boats," and we raced them in the water. We looked for tadpoles in standing water. We had a blast, and it didn't take any advanced planning or tools. Just stepping outside. Science proves this will do far more for your child's brain development than staring at any screen.

So how can we become more at home in nature and derive its benefits for ourselves and our families more often? It doesn't take much. You don't have to climb Everest, start backpacking every weekend, or travel to Japan. Just step outside. Maybe get a bird feeder and watch the birds. Learn what foods they like, what size birdhouses they need. Try to grow something. Sunflowers are easy. Walk the dog around the area. Notice the sounds, the sights. Is it always windy in the afternoon? From what direction does the wind blow? Step outside at night. Can you see the stars? Can you spot the constellation of Orion? Maybe you can ride a bike with the family after dinner. Maybe on the weekends you can go to an area to hike or stroll. Find a place with tree stumps, or a creek, or wildflowers. As my rainy day demonstrates, it doesn't take much to fascinate kids.

The goal of this book is to have you fall in love with and delight in God's handiwork and to discover His heart in it. The more you learn about the amazing things He has done, the more you want to learn and enjoy them. Ocean explorer Jacques Cousteau said, "We protect what we love." I remember the day my son was born. I held him in my arms with all that mama bear love gushing through my system and, with tears running down my face, I said to my husband, "I would jump in front of a *train* for this child." We protect what we love.

I want for you to fall so in love with this amazing, breathtaking world that you want to explore it and protect it. I want you to discover so many cool scientific and spiritual truths from nature that you want to share them with others. Then they too will fall in love with this world and want to safeguard it.

I want you to discover so many cool scientific
and spiritual truths from nature that you
want to share them with others.

You are not alone. You picked up this book because you love the outside world. The more I talk to people, read, and research, the more I realize there is a groundswell of quiet nature lovers. You may not be hugging trees or marching in the streets, but you care deeply about this beautiful world. You care about its health and the health of your family and future generations. You are part of a growing tribe of nature enthusiasts who realize it's important and life giving to get outside.

You wonder if anyone notices that spring is coming earlier and earlier each year. You feel overwhelmed about all the negative news about plastic in our oceans and drilling in the Arctic. I know I do. I want to lighten your load. I want to give you simple ways to delight in what God has made and then maybe take others along with you in your strolls outside. So that they too can smell and see the delights that a walk in the woods can provide. Hopefully, they too will discover the simple pleasures of identifying God's love notes in the skies—His songbirds. We want others to join us and realize there is a glorious world out there beyond the kitchen sink, cubicle, and car. And it is life giving to walk among what the Author of life has created.

Astronauts have a unique view of the earth. After seeing it from space, it affects their worldview, what they view as important. Kathy Sullivan, the first American woman to perform a space walk, returned to earth with a sense of awe for our fragile planet. "The thing that grew in me over these flights was a real motivation and desire... to not just enjoy these sights and take these pictures," she says, "but to make it matter." She says she never got tired of looking at Earth from the heavens. "I'm not sure I'd want to be in the same room with someone who could get tired of that."[3] In addition, she has a prescription for those of us who might have a jaundiced or arrogant view of the state of our earth: "If I could get every Earthling to do one circle of the Earth, I think things would run a little differently."[4]

God put so much creativity and wonder into this world. I want you to get a glimpse of it through these pages and hunger for more.

I've seen things deep underwater that most people in the world will never see, like those neon pink and purple sea slugs. Why did He do this? If hardly anyone was going to see it, why not make it gray and functional? He did it because it delights Him. He did it because He values what He makes.

And if He values all the tiny creatures in the Amazon rain forest and deep under the oceans, so should we. We have the erroneous notion about what the Genesis directive of *dominion* and *stewardship* means. Think of what dominion and stewardship mean in your relationship with your children. It means not poisoning them, not harming them for financial gain, not doing things that would stunt their growth. It's not too hard a concept to grasp, right?

Spending time in nature is healing. It can draw you closer to the creative heart of God. It can help anxiety. It can help ADHD. It can give you a new perspective. Spending time outside is good for your insides. It's no wonder that Beethoven, Einstein, and Steve Jobs all took long walks outside. It quieted their minds and fueled their creativity. In 1910, hiker and philosopher John Muir noted that we were a "tired, nerve-shaken, over-civilized people." We need to reconnect with nature now more than ever.

Spending time outside is good for your insides.

I want you to get outside more. You don't have to run a half marathon or become a master gardener. Just step outside your backdoor. I want you to have clean air to breathe, clean rivers and lakes and oceans for you and your children and grandchildren to play in. I want you to be able to look up at night and see the wondrous stars and spot the constellations. I want you to be able to pick out a deciduous tree from an evergreen. I want you to know a cardinal from a crow. I want you to be able to identify at least two different bird songs. I want you to hear the roar of wind in the forest and the peaceful lap of pond water on the side of a boat. I want you to thrill at the sight of a bear, bobcat, or banana slug. I want you to step outside and find the heart of God in nature. He spoke the world into existence and He continues to speak through His creation. He's there. He's everywhere. Just step outdoors, breathe deep, and fall in love with this outside life.

> Find the heart of God in nature...and fall
> in love with this outside life.

Exploring Further

1. Have you had a moment in nature where you felt restored, peaceful, awed by beauty? Where was that? Were you with anybody?

2. When is the last time you walked a forest trail, stomped in a puddle, or made a mud pie? If your answer is "a long time ago" or "never," explain what keeps you from spending more time outside.

3. What have your times in the outdoors taught you about God? If you have kids, take them on a walk and share this with them.

4. Does the call to explore and learn about creation make you nervous or excited?

1

All Creation Sings

Our boat rocked like a cradle in the gentle surge of the Maui cove. The captain of our whale watch expedition lowered the microphone deep into the water. Everyone on deck stopped murmuring, their eyes riveted to his hands. Sweat trickled down our necks and beaded on our upper lips in the late-morning sun as the boat rocked back and forth and water softly slapped the hull. We were hoping to hear the whales. Hoping to hear their otherworldly singsong chorus.

Every winter hundreds of humpback whales converge in the waters and bays around the Hawaiian Islands—particularly Maui. They come to these warm, protected bays to breed and give birth. What most delights tourists are the awesome breaches. This is when the whale leaps out of the water and crashes down like a three-story building toppling over. It's incredibly thrilling to see this up close, and it's not unusual to see tears in the eyes of most of the viewers on board once they've witnessed it.

Moments later a ribbon of sound spooled through the speakers. The eerie moaning, humming, longing, and up-and-down singsong of the humpback whale. We were transfixed. What were they saying? Why do they do that? Are they actually communicating with one another? Is it a territorial thing? Or do they like to hum and whistle just like we do? We peppered our captain with questions after he brought the microphone back on deck. But he had no answers—merely guesses.

Dr. Roger Payne of the Ocean Alliance has noted that the whales come up for air in such a way that it doesn't disturb their song. He speculates that this shows the singing is a conscious activity. He has also noted that a male singing will attract another male—not in a threatening, territorial way, but as a singing accompaniment. The other whale will join him, then go off and sing with different males. Scientists can only give educated guesses as to why whales sing. But sing they do.

With other animals, we have more information about why they vocalize. Frogs, antelope squirrels, birds, cicadas, and even toadfish make noises—or sing—to attract mates, warn of danger, or just because it's a hot August night. Other creatures, like bats and dolphins, use echolocation to bounce sound signals off objects to help direct them where to go or reveal more information about the size of an object.

What strikes me afresh when I consider the eerie song of the humpback whale or my favorite—the spiraling flute notes of the Swainson's thrush songbird—is that God didn't have to do this. Creating these creatures to sing was a conscious decision on His part. This fact—that many creatures "sing"—raises the question, *Why?* Why did He do it? Birds could still fly and exist without songs. Whales could still swim and breach without songs. So why did He do it? Was it just to thrill us? Was it just to delight Himself or us? I do know that the Genesis account, whether poetic metaphor or scientific timetable, depending on your view, records God's thoughts. He felt, after all that was made, "that it was good." He was pleased. So, apparently, it delighted Him. How extraordinary that He likes to delight us as well, and for that I am grateful.

We need to give voice to our gratitude, or else our hearts and minds forget. Why else would we repeat the Pledge of Allegiance as children every morning at school? It creates a well-worn neural pathway in our brains. Like a slide that millions of children have slid down. Or the deep grooves in the prairies from thousands of westward pioneers in covered wagons. It's almost impossible not to follow the path. For us school kids, the daily pledge was a well-trod course that was so deeply packed down with years of repeating, we could be standing on one foot, chewing gum, and doing minor math while reciting it. But rarely do we give voice to our blessings.

> We need to give voice to our gratitude,
> or else our hearts and minds forget.

Maybe we think it's old school. Or redundant. After all, if God knows our heart, what's the point? It's so much more expected and hip to whine about our schedules, our workloads, *the traffic*! and the myriad "hardships" that befall us as First World residents.

There is power in the spoken word. Perhaps that's why so many clubs, organizations, and secret societies make you recite their creeds, beliefs, and tenets so often. And maybe this is why, 30 years later, I still know the words to the doxology. We sang it almost every Sunday in church. This is the song that starts, "Praise God from whom all blessings flow…" Have you noticed that what you sing on Sunday tends to swirl around unbidden in your memory during the week? Giving voice, in words or song, wakes up our will and intention.

When our son was a toddler, I read parenting books voraciously. Some books advocated making your child say, "Yes, Mommy" after hearing a request. Apparently, research shows that what we utter with our lips, our physical bodies then obediently respond to. The mouth precedes the movement. And it worked. Stunningly. It was like we suddenly had this robotic son who would immediately get up when he spoke those words. It didn't last forever, but for a while the link between spoken agreement and obedient movement was almost freaky.

I find it natural and easy to express gratitude over nature's bounty. The fire-hot pink bougainvillea vine sprawling over the community center doorway always amazes me each year when it blooms. The lush, pulsating green hills after winter rains make me inhale their fertile smell with appreciation. I easily say out loud, "Thank You, God! This is magnificent!" When I'm crunching along a carpet of blazing fall leaves, my heart swells with gratitude, and I whisper, "Thank You." When I pluck a sun-warmed blackberry off the vine in the late afternoon and taste exploding summer sweetness, I close my eyes in reverence. When I'm hiking along a mountain trail and hear a meadowlark or the wind rushing through the pines, I'm so grateful to be alive and experiencing it that tears come to my eyes.

> When I pluck a sun-warmed blackberry off the vine in the late afternoon and taste exploding summer sweetness, I close my eyes in reverence.

What is not so easy for me is to sing in heavy, anxious seasons. To be intentionally, demonstratively, verbally grateful and thankful when times are tough and confusing. When I was going through seven years of infertility, when my father was dying, when family members got divorced, I wasn't singing.

Yet I've noticed that no matter what tragedy has befallen the world—wars, famines, family job losses, or deaths—the birds still sing. They sing no matter what. It seems incongruous to wake up and hear their joyful dawn song. When disease chews relentlessly upon innocent children, when good people lose their jobs, when family and friends are mowed down by rampant and senseless evil, the last thing on our minds is to sing. Much less, to be grateful. That's why Tammy Trent's story is so mesmerizing to me.

She and her husband met at a church youth group in their teens. They went on to have a fairy-tale marriage, and he constantly left her notes about how much he loved her. He was continually focused on being a man of God. They worked together as a team on her burgeoning career as a national singer. Life couldn't be sweeter.

His hobby was free diving. This is where you don't use scuba tanks but hold your breath while diving deep underwater. They went on a picture-perfect vacation to the Caribbean, where he put on his wet suit, dove into the water, and never came back up again. Ever.

Shell-shocked and stunned with grief, her first response was to pray an "I trust You, God" prayer. Then, while packing up their clothes, alone in her hotel room, a maid heard her crying and asked to pray with her. They ended up clutching each other, sobbing and singing a praise song together.

I don't know about you, but if I were in her shoes, I don't think a praise song would be the first thing on my lips—much less with a perfect stranger. I've never understood those people who say, "Oh, I wasn't mad at God when my daughter was raped and murdered." Really? He who stills the wind and sun and could have stopped the monster from harming your daughter but didn't, and you're not mad? I relate more to people like my friend Chris. We were on a walk the other day when she said, "I'm not one of those Christians that came out of the womb saying, 'Thy will be done.'"

But I *would* like to get there. To be like one of them. To be on God's "A" team.

I guess that's what our time on earth is all about. Sort of a boot camp or prep school for eternity. Some of us have to take remedial courses on sovereignty, grace, mercy, and faith over and over again. Some of us have one huge decision in a moment of time. We all, at some point, have to choose in the dark whether we will curse or sing.

When the Bible says, "Rejoice in the Lord always. I will say it again: Rejoice! Let your gentleness be evident to all" (Philippians 4:4-5), we roll our eyes and think, *That's easy when the money is flowing and life is sweet.* So were we told this just to torture us? Just to mock our pain?

> We all, at some point, have to choose in the dark whether we will curse or sing.

Most people think of the book of Job and think "pain and suffering." We say that someone has the "patience of Job" when we refer to enduring hard times. But there is another side to the coin. In the midst of Job's suffering and misery and asking, "Why, God?" God points to something else: the beauty of His creation. His manifold greatness and creativity and outright joy in the natural world.

> Where were you when I laid the earth's foundation?
> Tell me, if you understand.
> Who marked off its dimensions? Surely you know!
> Who stretched a measuring line across it?
> On what were its footings set,
> or who laid its cornerstone—

while the morning stars sang together
and all the angels shouted for joy?

Who shut up the sea behind doors
when it burst forth from the womb,
when I made the clouds its garment
and wrapped it in thick darkness,
when I fixed limits for it
and set its doors and bars in place,
when I said, "This far you may come and no farther;
here is where your proud waves halt"?...

Have you journeyed to the springs of the sea
or walked in the recesses of the deep?
Have the gates of death been shown to you?
Have you seen the gates of the deepest darkness?...

Can you bind the chains of the Pleiades?
Can you loosen Orion's belt?
Can you bring forth the constellations in their seasons
or lead out the Bear with its cubs?
Do you know the laws of the heavens?
Can you set up God's dominion over the earth?
(Job 38:4-11,16-17,31-33).

To some, this could seem egotistical and sort of a rubbing-it-in-your-face moment from God in the midst of suffering. Job is crying out, "Why?" And God seems to be saying, "Dude! Have you noticed My amazing work in creation?" I mentioned this to my husband, Tom, and he commented, "Well, it only seems harsh if you're prideful. If you believe you deserve something else. Something other, or better." *Here we go again,* I thought.

I've walked through this territory before with Tom. When I was telling him that I thought God was a jerk through those seven years in the fertility desert, he pointed out the error in my point of reference. "You think you deserve better, but actually, you deserve death due to your missing the mark—sinning every day. We live in mercy. God doesn't owe you anything."

So when we're humble, God's wonders and creation can give confidence and comfort. But not if we're proud. His power, creativity, and majesty can inspire confidence and comfort or confusion and a critical spirit. Our choice.

> When we're humble, God's wonders and creation
> can give confidence and comfort.

Of all the sins mentioned in the Bible (and there's quite a list: murder, lying, adultery, stealing, and coveting, to name a few), the worst one is pride. Most of us would laugh at this. *Pride?* That quiet little voice inside that tells you, *You're better than this. You're better than the rest of them, and you* deserve *more.* That is worse than murder? To put it into perspective, the religious leaders' pride is what led to the crucifixion of Jesus Christ. Pride is what led Satan to think himself equal to God. Pride is the cornerstone of it all. It may be hidden in our hearts, quietly scheming and thinking, but it's still lethal.

Pride is particularly lethal because it blinds us. It blinds us to the wondrous blessings right in front of us and tells us, *You're missing out on what could be better.* Pride tells us, *You* deserve *better!* No, we don't. We deserve death. We can't get through a day without sinning against neighbors, our God, and ourselves. We are blind to the kaleidoscope of crazy-beautiful and outrageous riches that surround us daily. I think about this when I read a biography of someone who has to deal with blindness, deafness, quadriplegia, or whatever. I can see a breathtaking sunset. I can hear the roar of the wind through the trees. I can hike a trail. If I choose to, I can focus on my blessings and be grateful instead of looking over the fence and whining, believing I deserve better.

Although we go through painful times, God is still great and good. One reality doesn't negate the other. And as David said in the Psalms, "This I know, that God is *for* me" (Psalm 56:9 NASB, emphasis mine). He is on our side; He has our best interests at heart. And when we are humble and not blinded by pride, we can see and appreciate His blessings.

God is in charge, and He operates out of love because He *is* love. Whether or not we understand it. No matter how bleak and dark the moment is. The point is, in our blackest moments of confusion and pain, to offer it up to Him. To give voice to our condition, whether grace filled and grateful or sinful and seedy, as a step of faith—although we can't see the outcome—is defiantly faithful. That thought is delicious to me—to be defiantly faithful. It's as if I'm telling the devil, "Forget it, dude. No way you are having my heart!" The world calls this whistling in the dark. God calls it a sacrifice of praise. And it's music to His ears.

> God is in charge, and He operates out of
> love because He *is* love.

Every day, every morning, all creation sings. Whether a disaster has just hit or a life is falling apart bit by bit. With songs of praise, the walls of Jericho fell down. With songs about the faithfulness of God, Paul and Silas miraculously escaped prison. There is power in the spoken and sung word. Up in the heavens, down in the forests, and deep under the sea, all creation sings. Let's join in.

Exploring Further

1. Read this passage from Zephaniah 3:17:

> The Lord your God is with you,
>   the Mighty Warrior who saves.
> He will take great delight in you;
>   in his love he will no longer rebuke you,
>   but will rejoice over you with singing.

How does this make you feel? Is it hard to believe, or a relief?

2. What are ways that people in your life have—or are—"singing" over you? Or maybe with you?

3. Read Psalm 65:5-8:

> You answer us with awesome and righteous deeds,
>   God our Savior,
> the hope of all the ends of the earth
>   and of the farthest seas,
> who formed the mountains by your power,
>   having armed yourself with strength,
> who stilled the roaring of the seas,
>   the roaring of their waves,
>   and the turmoil of the nations.
> The whole earth is filled with awe at your wonders;
>   where morning dawns, where evening fades,
>   you call forth songs of joy.

When has God's hope awed you during a time of pride or disappointment?

4. What about God's creation or works in your life do you feel are worth singing about?

2

White-Water Rafting

Crystalline snowflakes pirouette in leisurely descent from the slate-gray heavens. Quiet as cat whiskers, they settle upon the shoulders of the California Sierra Mountains in a cottony white coverlet. Around Lake Tahoe, not far from the 1960 Olympic Games in Squaw Valley, the snowpack gradually increases. Like a layer cake, the snow builds up over the winter months to a depth of 25 to 41 feet. It is silent, beautiful, fortune building, and deadly. This is the area that entombed the pioneer Donner party in 1846 for four months under relentless snowstorms, starving them, and forcing them to resort to cannibalism.

In 1848 it brought fortune. Along the American River, whose snowmelt scoured out mountain canyons, James Marshall discovered gold at Sutter's Mill. The great Gold Rush was on, and people from all over the world raced to California to become millionaires. Today, the only gold to be found is in harnessing the power of snowmelt and its resulting vigorous river during the spring and summer thaw.

To ski resorts, urban centers, and thirsty farms downstream, monstrous snowstorms and deep snowpacks are the stuff of dreams. Their fortunes and success are tied to the amount of snow that falls. It means business and prosperity. As spring temperatures warm up, this snowpack begins to melt, creating small rivulets that feed downward into the north, south, and middle forks of the American River, supporting the voracious appetites of water consumers and white-water rafting companies.

We were a motley crew. All of us single twentysomethings from church were looking for a fun weekend of white-water rafting in the middle of a searing July summer. Standing around in don't-care-if-it-gets-ruined T-shirts and shorts, we warily eyed the river. Like most in our group, I had never rafted before. We had entrusted our lives not to an established rafting company and professional guide, but to a friend of a friend. We huddled together on the banks of the river listening to his instructions, assessing his trustworthiness, while fingering our rented, unfamiliar equipment of paddles, life vests, and rafts.

"If you fall out," he warned, "but you probably won't; but if you do, make sure you orient yourself so your feet are facing ahead of you. Get your feet in front of you—go downstream feet first. Whatever you do, you don't want to crack your head on the rocks. That's just gonna be smashing pumpkins time. You can't fight the river—go with it—and hopefully we can pick you up downstream. Just make sure you go feet first."

Looking at the wild water careening around boulders the size of houses, I understood why. To hit one of those headfirst (we didn't have helmets) would mean arriving home in a body bag. The admonishments of our guide seemed sensible, but I had no intention of practicing my swimming skills feet first. I intended to be planted securely in the raft.

We pushed off, and while I was hoping we'd start with baby rapids, sort of hang out on the edges of the torrent where the water seemed calmer, we learned that to safely get around the boulders, we needed to be in the center of the current, where it's moving the swiftest and feels wildest and out of control. We also learned we are not in the raft to coast and take it easy. All hands are needed to paddle furiously, to work with the current and keep us in the right position to navigate the obstacles.

It was a glorious, exhilarating, roller-coaster ride of splashing hilarity. We worked together like furious Polynesians, paddling until our arms ached, while laughing and whooping with delight. It was both terrifying and outrageously fun, and when we abandoned ourselves to his leadership, we trusted our guide implicitly. He'd been here before, and we hadn't. When he barked out, "Paddle hard to the right!" we strained as one and whipsawed around boulders.

It's all fun and games until someone gets tossed. That someone would be me. One moment I was riding in adrenaline-charged, screaming hilarity, and the next I was dumped into icy water and unable to catch my breath.

As a collegiate swimmer, I usually feel quite at home in the water. But this was nothing like the placid pools and languid lakes I was used to. It was a stun gun to the system. The air punched out of my lungs. I kept spitting, gasping, opening my mouth wider like a landed fish in hope of sucking air into my withered lungs. The ice water in my face didn't bother me as much as the body-numbing cold. The icy, just-melted snow immobilized my thoughts and responses. With my life preserver on, my head was somewhat above the churning water, and my frozen brain synapses could only focus on one thought: "Feet first! Feet first! Whatever you do, keep your feet in front of you!"

When we get tossed overboard into the tumult
of life, we can still choose to listen to voices of
encouragement instead of voices of discouragement.

While gulping air and blinking water out of my eyes, I could see massive boulders ahead and concentrated my whole being on orienting my feet in front of me. "Feet first!" I kept chanting to myself as the river bucked, churned, and tried to spin me off course. To fight the flow would have been crazy suicide. My best bet was to stay in the middle of the galloping current and careen around the rocks. I knew people had died on this river, sucked under the boulders, pinned by the massive force of the rapids. I was trying not to completely freak out. I could dimly hear the shouts of others over the roaring river, and the screaming fears swimming in my head. But without hope of rescue and feeling abandoned to the river's force, I completely laser-focused on those two words I believed would save me—"Feet first!"

When you're chucked in the midst of life's tumult, you are usually utterly alone. Others can call instructions to you, they can commiserate with you, but they can't fix you. They can't stop the circumstances. They are on a distant shore, literally and figuratively. And the raging torrent around and, greater still, inside of you intensifies your feelings of being completely cut off.

It is here you must focus to hear the one voice that will save you. Will you listen to inner voices of defeat and unworthiness? "You idiot, how did you end up here?" Or voices of encouragement and hope? "This will be okay. Just stay focused and follow his instructions."

Thoughts of "this isn't fair" were useless to me. And my personal favorite, "Why me?" would never be answered, nor would it help me. (If I had understood the physics of what catapulted me out of the raft, would it make the immediate danger any less?) I had to deal with what was at that moment, and choose my response.

My friend Amanda was jolted with fear when she discovered her husband had a porn addiction. While her initial feelings were fear, nausea, and fury, and her instinctive thoughts were to rage, punish, and blame, she chose a different response. "I cried with him," she said. "He was miserable, feeling trapped, and I was miserable too. What good would it do to accuse and blame?" Amanda chose to focus on the positive: He asked for help! So she and her husband found a faith-based, compassionate counselor and worked on ways to get him out of the pit.

When it smacks us in the face that someone we love is addicted, and we feel like we are drowning in despair, we always have a choice in our response. Blame, drama, and guilt are as helpful as anvils to a jogger. It just weighs them down with extra baggage they can't possibly manage if they are to move forward. I love what Al-Anon says: "You didn't cause it, you can't control it, and you can't cure it." This is a useful refrain for most situations where other people's behaviors are resulting in our losing our equilibrium and triggering the avalanche of blame, guilt, and hysteria.

Sometimes, we have to choose to "faith it 'til we make it." To their face, we do not freak out. We act poised. (Every parent of teenagers knows this tactic.) "No, this doesn't diminish my love for you. Yes, we need to do something—getting help would be a good idea." We try to project a facade of preternatural calm so as not to add gasoline to an already volatile situation. And often, acting "as if" helps make it so. Our hearts and brains start behaving in accordance with our actions.

Most of us respond to the moments of raging mayhem in our lives as a nightmare from which we want immediate relief. "Stop it! Stop it now! Oh, God, I know You can. Please *stop* it!" This is our knee-jerk prayer. But these times can also be an upside-down, inside-out gift.

This sort of tumult forces us to focus on the truth we know and grab on to it for dear life. In the midst of life's storms, focusing on *Who*, not *what*, will save you. Ever notice how your prayer life improves when all other routes are closed off? The comforts of friends, position, pride, and material blessings won't help us in times like these. Like a mariner caught in a storm, dropping his anchors and relying on their weight and drag, we must trust all our weight to what will hold us—or, as believers, Who will hold us.

In the midst of life's storms, focusing on *Who*,
not *what*, will save you.

It's easy to sit in our houses of worship and nod in acquiescence to doctrine and three teachable points. But how we react in tough times is the real measure of our faith. It shows where we are willing to put the weight of our future, and what we believe will hold us. Our behavior will reveal who or what we have been listening to and truly believe. Our actions expose our innermost thoughts.

When I was desperate after seven years of infertility to get pregnant, I was absolutely tempted when someone told me, "There's a statue in Mexico that if you touch it, you'll get pregnant. It's worked for hundreds of women!" While that sounds bizarre, idiotic, and somewhat voodoo-ish, it did flicker across my mind, "What could it hurt?" A cursory glimpse of Genesis through Malachi would answer: a lot. More specifically, the first commandment: "You shall have no other gods before me" (Exodus 20:3). When you're desperate, even the sacrilegious can sound sane. Although I was tempted, my anchor of belief held sway, and I turned away from trusting in that option. When I hear a posturing pastor railing against various sins, and afterward discover he is as ensnared as those he is demonizing, I know one thing for sure. His position and authority is the anchor—the utmost priority—in his life. He is resting all his weight on that, not on humility before God.

When my life is swirling out of control, and I'm failing at controlling events or my tongue, my morning alone time with God suddenly gets waaaaay more priority than before. I'm no saint. I've just learned the hard way. It's like I cannot...function...without...Him. My prayers are offered through sodden tissues. I'm devouring my Bible. I'm embarrassed to admit it, but there it is. Tough times help me focus and listen to His voice like never before. Tough times sweep me into His presence. And there is where I finally secure the peace and direction I so desperately need. There is where the waves stand still.

In that freezing uproar of rapids, our rafting guide's admonition to go feet first was the only thing my mind could grasp. I didn't know how long I would be there. I didn't know if I would make it downstream. I didn't know if anyone would help me—or just whiz on by, unable to fight the current themselves. But one thing I could do: I could get my feet in front of me.

I aligned myself with the current, whipping safely around a set of small boulders (whew!), and I could hear my friend Laura screaming my name from the raft. Good. That meant they might be nearby, but I couldn't turn and look without getting tumbled under and spun off course. With my teeth chattering and my body shaking all over, I was focused on the words of our guide—staying in the current, feet first.

After what felt like a half hour—but what was probably a few minutes—our leader had maneuvered next to me, grabbed the back of my life jacket, hoisted me out of the churning madness, and plunked me into the raft. I marveled at how he was able to do that while still guiding the raft through rapids. But I didn't have time to ponder or be pampered. "Paddle!" he yelled. So I scrambled for my paddle, dug into the churning water, and joined in with the others.

I love sucking the marrow out of life in the great outdoors. I delight in God's creative work in the astounding world He has made. And in this outside life, you can have plenty of amazing adventures. But there is that other side of the coin.

Jesus said, "In the world you have tribulation, but take courage; I have overcome the world" (John 16:33 NASB). Other versions say you will have "trouble" or "many trials and sorrows." The gist is, it's not all fun and games here on this beautiful earth. Life happens. Unfairness happens. Tragedies happen. But Jesus is pointing out that He is the source of our peace, our victory over circumstances, the Who—not the what—in this scary and crazy adventure of life.

We operate as if we can control most of the events of our lives. And if we can't, our money, technology, or science will. But for the guy yesterday who got killed by a freak boulder crashing down the mountainside and smashing his car, and my friend who has an incurable disease, this is erroneous thinking. In reality, there's much of life we cannot control. The best we can do is stop our illusion of control and get in the main flow, work with it, and enjoy the ride. And if we want victory over our inevitable twists and turns, we listen to His words. Focusing on the Who, not the what, will bring us peace. That's an anchor He promised would hold.

Exploring Further

1. When have you felt chucked out of your comfort zone and into a crazy situation?
2. What thoughts and feelings went through your mind?
3. Were you irritated or angry at anyone as a result?
4. What brought you comfort? Did you find a way to God's presence and peace?

3

Adventure

This is a good place to find auger shells," Chuck said as he adjusted his scuba gear. "I've found lots at the bottom of this shipping channel." And then he jumped into the water.

What? I'm going scuba diving in a shipping channel? Isn't that crazy stupid? Visions of giant propellers sucking me up and churning me into chum filled my head. But Chuck—the only other diver on this gig—was already descending to the depths, so I jumped in after him.

I had stopped in Pago Pago, American Samoa, on one of my annual trips home while living in Australia. My aim was always to try a different country or location for scuba diving to and from Down Under. Chuck was a scuba shop owner I hired to take me diving. In his sixties, he had more energy than me and apparently wasn't fazed about diving the shipping channel leading into the harbor at Pago Pago.

On the sandy bottom at 160 feet deep, Chuck dug his hand into ripples in the sand and pulled up several auger shells, three to five inches long. They were cream colored with dark markings, and resembled a narwhal-like tusk, their conical shape ending in a menacing point. How had he known just where they would be? With sign language, he pointed out to me their narrow, furrowed paths, like plowed rows in the seabed. Where each path ended, you'll find an auger. I gleefully followed his example and began my own quest of finding their trails and tracking their whereabouts.

While I was delighted with the shells, the back of my mind was screaming, *You're too deep! You're too deep! Surface! Surface! Now!* Nitrogen narcosis is a serious threat when you dive too deep. And "too deep" is different for different people. The five-foot woman of 100 pounds will have a different physical response than the 180-pound man at six feet tall. Everyone has a different level of susceptibility. When scuba diving, you are breathing the air we all breathe, which is composed of a mixture of oxygen, nitrogen, and trace amounts of carbon dioxide, argon, and other gases. But the deeper you go, the more you are affected by the nitrogen. And deeper than 100 feet is definitely the danger zone. It's like drunk diving, which can lead to euphoria, overconfidence, and stupid decisions. Or, to be blunt, death.

As excited as I was about my new skill of tracking augers and discovering them, I was worried about suffering the effects of being down too deep for too long. But I had enough sense to snare a few.

Years later, those shells sit in a glass vase at the top of my bookcase. When I look at them, I smile. They remind me of diving in tropical Samoa and all the other delightful discoveries of that trip I went on by myself in pursuit of adventure.

This is in contrast to the slightly icky feeling I have when I look at fake shells. Or those I've purchased for decorative purposes. It's not that the shells are ugly or not as nice as the ones I've gathered on my journeys; it's that they are bereft of memory and meaning. There are no adventures or achievements associated with them. Almost as if they are falsely saying, "I represent sunny vacations in exotic locations!" And they don't. They represent pretend adventures. They were purchased and have no intrinsic value to me. It feels sort of like cheating.

It's the same distaste I feel when I hear about pretend Vietnam vets. Those guys who purchase medals at flea markets and then pawn themselves off as some sort of war hero. They are faux warriors with no real memories of action. They are pretending to be something they are not.

This is why I start twitching when I see my tween-ager preferring video game quests as opposed to real, outdoor adventures. I don't care how many levels he ascends or quests he accomplishes in Game Land; it isn't the same by a long shot. It is pretend adventure. *Distaste* is a mild word for what dances across my mind. I seethe inside when I compare these fake pursuits to my vivid memories of childhood bike rides, canoe trips, swimming afternoons, and outdoor explorations.

> I start twitching when I see my tween-ager preferring video game quests as opposed to real, outdoor adventures.

What I want to say is, "What kind of lame excuse is *this* for real adventure? This is a total waste of your mind, talents, and body. Go ride a bike; go for a walk. Get your sofa-loving self *outside!*" But instead, I adopt the calm attitude of a totally saintly mother and say, "Sweetheart, it's so nice outside. Would you like to join me for a walk?"

He, of course, says, "No, I would not like to." And then I respond with the magical formula of threats and bribes. (If you don't go for a walk with me, you must surrender your phone. If you do go, we'll stop by the frozen yogurt place.) Although I feel like a complete failure as a mother who is an outdoor writer, I've accomplished my goal: He is outside and getting some vitamin D.

Young men used to have opportunities for adventure. They could join the other men in the community for hunting down meat. They would be taught how to flush out the game, how to use their weapons, and how to prepare the animal for carrying home. Or even just to work side by side with their fathers to learn carpentry or automotive repair skills to make them productive and self-sufficient. But today, despite Boy Scouts or organized sports, there is little opportunity for a young man to feel like he's scaling the summit, accomplishing something significant, contributing to the community, much less slaying a dragon. So the instant fix of the artificial accomplishments of video games is hard to resist.

While I might be hard on him for substituting pretend adventures for real ones, I'm uncomfortably aware that I'm often guilty of the same thing in regard to my faith. Don't I prefer to read stirring biographies of others as opposed to stepping out and wildly trusting God on my own? Am I not guilty of recommending that people read about the faith of George Müller, the forgiveness of Corrie ten Boom, the daring of Brother Andrew, and the sacrificial love of Katie Davis, while neglecting to mimic their Christlike example? Yeah, absolutely.

Why? Because I second-guess that I could ever do what these people have done. I'm brought to tears by the stories of George Müller, who never asked for donations but merely prayed and sought God for the resources for his orphanages. His answers to prayer were multimillion dollar, supernatural, and faith building (something that's rare today with "send money now to support us" pleas and building funds). Corrie ten Boom's experiences in the Nazi death camps are harrowing, and her forgiveness of Nazi tormentors even more challenging to my secret grudges. Brother Andrew's accounts of smuggling Bibles into hostile countries are gutsy and stirring—so why can't I talk to my neighbor? And Katie Davis shows us what it's like to take Jesus at His word, leave the stuff behind, embrace Africa's orphans, and truly feed His sheep. (I'm trying not to think about my clothes closet.)

All these believers relied on the same God; they had no more or no less ability than we do. God loves us the same as He loves them. But there is a difference. They took God at His word. They were willing to run with what Scripture says: "Go and make disciples."

My first response isn't always to take a step forward in faith. Like an armchair adventurer who loves to read about climbing mountains, running rapids, or tracking down rare birds, all too often I do settle for reading about and weeping over someone else's spiritual adventure rather than experiencing my own.

We forget that God's adventure doesn't have to mean going somewhere exotic or necessarily doing anything extraordinary. It can be as simple as inviting our neighbors to church or telling our coworkers why we have hope. God leads us all into individualized itineraries suited to our personalities and preferences.

Why are we so afraid? Why do we settle for reading about, talking about, but not stepping into our own adventures of faith? It's almost as if we have an automatic response: "That's nice for them, but I don't believe God has called me to (fill in the blank)." Or even if we did drop everything and step out, I'm betting that many of us wonder, *Would He come through for me too? Would He show up just as powerfully for me?*

We suffer doubt and unbelief. We think our past and our current lukewarm faith are not worthy of God blessing us the way He did those daring adventurers. But this is wrong thinking. Our past sins and misadventures do not disqualify us for God's adventures. He's not finished with us yet.

"No eye has seen, no ear has heard, and no mind has imagined what God has prepared for those who love him" (1 Corinthians 2:9 NLT).

Our past sins and misadventures do not disqualify us for God's adventures. He's not finished with us yet.

King David was an adulterer. The apostle Paul was a murderer. God has used prostitutes as well. He can and will take anyone on an adventure. We just have to be available.

We can start small. I didn't start scuba diving by jumping in and plunging below 100 feet. I signed up for classes, learned the math for depth and time spent diving, took small, easy dips first. Then I was ready for big adventures all around the South Pacific islands.

Katie Davis started small by helping orphaned children in Africa on a short-term mission trip in high school. After a taste of how rewarding that was, she hungered for more. She went back ("just for a while") and eventually moved there, adopted 13 girls, and started a foundation. God didn't plop a gigantic, overwhelming plan in her lap. Her path was revealed step-by-step. As she saw God move, she took another step. Her faith walk is as adventurous and exciting as any Mount Everest account. And while it's not without heartaches and unanswered prayers, her journey is far more meaningful and has eternal value—the rescuing of orphaned souls.

My father-in-law was the pastor of a small church in Pennsylvania. They lived by faith. My husband, Tom, watched his parents pray and then see God deliver a bag of potatoes or chickens to their backdoor. Despite having no savings account, his parents always fed the homeless and believed God would provide. Taking bigger steps of faith than I am comfortable with is easy for my husband because he was trained for it. He savors the thrill and adventure in stepping out and expecting God to deliver. He once invited a homeless guy living in an ambulance to come move in with him. This man, Steve, taught Tom guitar and went on to become a pastor. Tom has no problem considering this again for our family; I have no problem imagining robbery and slit throats. Some faith journeys make me catch my breath.

> Taking bigger steps of faith is easy for my husband because he was trained for it. He savors the thrill and adventure in stepping out and expecting God to deliver.

I do love adventures: Moving to another country by myself? No worries! Ziplining hundreds of feet in the air? Totally fun! Scuba diving? Absolutely! White-water rafting? Love it! But I'm more tentative when it comes to being adventurous in my faith. So while my faith journey isn't as daring as my wilderness excursions, I'm in training to take bigger leaps. Our family teaches a Bible study to middle school kids at our local church. I speak up more now when people are deriding Christians. I try to challenge the knee-jerk judgment of the political diversity around us. I want to turn climate change debates into discussions about creation care. Our family is looking into opportunities to use our vacation time to go on a mission trip to serve others. Because I don't want to meet Jesus at the end of my life and say, "I didn't have the guts to trust You. I didn't live out my faith full of adventure and significance; I settled for pretend adventures by reading about others' accounts of daring trust."

It's easy to seek outdoor adventures, and it's even easier to read about someone else's feats of daring. But the historical record shows that faith adventures—in which we really step out and trust God—prove ultimately to be more satisfying and soul stirring.

Exploring Further

1. What adventures have you had in life? Or what adventures would you like to try?

2. Do you know someone who had a faith adventure, or have you read about someone else's faith adventure that you really admire?

3. What did you admire about them? Is there any way you could apply that to your life?

4. Read John 14:12. Do you think Jesus meant this for us today? Why or why not?

4

Chipmunk

The geese overhead gave their mournful, signature signal that autumn was upon us. Flying in military precision across the cobalt Wisconsin sky, they honked out their farewell. My mother's patio was covered with gold and russet leaves as I sat on the lounge chair reading my book and reveling in the crisp air.

I heard him before I saw him. Leaves under the bushes rustled, and the branches above him jerked slightly. Then, a tiny pink nose surrounded by whiskers that twitched with nervous energy appeared under a leaf. Two dark, glossy eyes accented with what looked like white eyeliner peered out. He was after the bird seed. It lay sprinkled on the ground just a few feet in front of him, having been scattered by the birds above in the feeder. He ventured out a bit further from beneath his covering. Tiny ears and a tan body, with striking black and white stripes just along his back, emerged. With his furry tail standing straight up in the air, he darted forward and started stuffing his cheeks with bird seed.

The birds hopping on the ground didn't pay him any attention. His delicate little paws scooped up bits and stuffed and stuffed and stuffed endless piles of seed into his cheek pouches. As they began to expand outward, I started giggling at his absurd appearance. He sat up on his hind legs and looked toward me, his cheeks defying physics and bulging out beyond his body width. It looked like he had swallowed a Pink Pearl eraser horizontally and was about to topple over. Instead, he dashed back under the bushes with his hoard.

Soon, he returned. This time darting around underneath the peanut feeder. Again, the frantic stuffing-stuffing-stuffing with his delicate paws, and again the comical cheeks ballooned out before he scurried off to his secret lair. Although they are rodents, and although I told my son when he wanted a pet rat, "This mama don't do rodents!!" I find chipmunks adorable. While squirrels are the nemesis of bird lovers and their bird feeders, chipmunks are smaller, absurdly cute, and pose not much of a threat. My mother affectionately called him "My little chippie" when he was about.

Chipmunks are found throughout most of the United States and Canada, and their ability to overstuff, cram, and jam their cheeks full of food is remarkable. These cheek pouches serve dual purposes. They allow them to quickly gather food, but more importantly, they serve as sort of a suitcase for temporary storage and transport while they carry food to safe locations of shelter. One chipmunk who was caught and examined was found to have over 1000 cinnamon bush seeds stuffed in his cheeks. Others that have been livetrapped were found to contain oats, wheat, and nuts as well. Chipmunks aren't the only mammals that have this ability to overstuff their cheek pouches. The platypus, some monkeys, and hamsters do too. When you see a hamster or a chipmunk with their cheek pouches bursting, they give you a visual picture for the smorgasbord idiom of "stuffing your face."

So why do they need to stuff their cheeks, scurry about, and hide their food? Because they live haunted by lack. Chipmunks hibernate during the winter, and unlike other mammals (like bears) that live off of their stored fat, chipmunks need to have food put away so they can periodically eat their stored cache of food throughout the winter. Their burrows are usually underground with several concealed entrances and constructed quite neatly with separate areas for sleeping, food, and refuse. This is probably why they are classified under the genus Tamias, which is Greek for "treasurer," "steward," or "housekeeper."

And since they are solitary critters (except for mating season), they alone are responsible for sourcing, stuffing, and stashing their food supplies. It's crucial to their survival. While I find their overstuffed cheeks adorable and their hoarding habits admirable, it's not so cute when humans do it. I know this because I sort of have earned a black belt in stuffing my life full of things I don't need. And trust me, my husband doesn't find it adorable or admirable when he can barely open our closet door to access his clothes.

I put together an embarrassing list of all the ways I stuff my life out of a mistaken, haunting sense of lack—much like our chipmunk. Maybe you can relate to some of these.

Clothes. Look what's in my in-box. A sale on my favorite jeans! And now they come in brown. That's hard to find. I am always on the lookout for brown. I like to pair it with blush pink and turquoise. This is the one brand that fits me well and doesn't make my backside look like the broadside of a barn. I will wear them forever, and besides, they might discontinue this style. One more pair couldn't hurt, and it is half off! Plus, I'm sure I can match them with several other items, so it's really a smart buying decision. I can click on this ad and have them delivered to my door. (And maybe stash them in the closet before anyone notices.)

Reality. My closet is smashed, crammed, and overstuffed with clothes. I have apparel from my skinny years through to my hefty years. Right now I'm in between, so if and when I venture back into either of my former categories, those clothes will be old and out of style. Best to donate them and let others enjoy them now.

Food. I'm tense. I'm worried about my husband's job, my son, my deadlines. I pace around a bit and pass by the refrigerator. I remember that some leftover lasagna is in there. It's nine o'clock in the morning, and I've had breakfast, but I'm starving! Well, at least it feels that way. Logically, I know I am not starving, but I feel frantic for food. I pull out the lasagna and, standing in front of the refrigerator (with the door still open), I plunge a fork into the welcoming cushion of pasta, tomato sauce, and gooey goodness it offers. *Bliss.* Now for something sweet to finish it off… I think there's some stashed Halloween candy in the back of this pantry. A Tootsie Roll!. I'm not that into them, but hey, it's chocolate and has sugar. I stuff it into my mouth. I don't even register what I'm eating as my jaws methodically and with machine-like precision masticate the sugary treat. My eyes dart around the kitchen to see if there is something more satisfying with a bigger sugar smack. Toast with honey? I know I'm not hungry, but I don't care. I feel an urgent need to stuff my face.

Reality. I am eating out of stress. I have no physical hunger for food, but I'm using the contents of the refrigerator to medicate my feelings of fear and lack of talent, and to stuff down anxiety over things I can't control. I should step outside and go for a brief walk to clear my mind and heart.

Crafts. "I could make that" is the crafter's siren call. It's the Achilles' heel to making my life productive in areas that really matter for eternity. And I fall prey to the siren call most of the time. Embroidery yarn kits, needlepoint projects, paints, sewing fabric and notions, knitting and crocheting essentials, jewelry supplies—I have it all. All stuffed into our garage and in my master closet. Projects I swear I will finish, and promising opportunities to make glorious gifts for others. (And I have made some amazing things over the years.) These supplies cost a lot of money. I can't just chuck them out. Think of the money I will save by not buying presents but instead making them! I love working with my hands. I love making items for others. Is that such a bad thing? I cram another skein of sock yarn into the drawer. This will be a pair of socks that someone will cherish.

Reality. I would have to live to be 120 years old before I would realistically get through all of these supplies. And cleaning out my mother's house showed me that nobody will care after I'm gone about all the hours I put into each project. It made me wince knowing what effort she put into every craft project, but we simply couldn't find a home for all of it. We tried. I'm pained to admit, some of it was tossed. Do I really want to invest hours into something that my kinfolk might dump into the trash? Maybe I could focus on just one or two crafts and donate the rest.

Beauty products. They are always coming out with new technology to make us look better. Really, it's truly amazing all the scientific breakthroughs in skin care. This evening cream? It has green tea extract. This promises to tackle the free radicals in my skin (never mind I'm not sure what those are, but I'm sure it's *muy mal* for my skin!). There's also this foundation sample I got as a free gift for buying perfume. The packaging says it has sunscreen (yay!) and hyaluronic acid—which will plump up my skin, erase wrinkles, and make me look dewy, fresh, and amazing. Never mind that the color isn't quite right, and it makes me look somewhat like a traditional Japanese geisha in a pale mask. It would be expensive to buy. It's the latest technology. So I stuff it in with the rest of the mismatched lipsticks, blush, perfume samples, and odds and ends collected over time. I have quite a selection of valuable (expensive) makeup!

Reality. Makeup, like food, gets nasty over time. Any product that I haven't used in six months should be tossed. Any product I don't use regularly should be thrown out, thus liberating all the minutes I spend sorting through the mass of products that have robbed me of free time. Plus, less is more. I don't want to end up looking like a desperate older woman with too much makeup on. I need to stop thinking of it as throwing valuable things away and think of it as freeing up valuable time.

These are just a few areas where I stuff, stuff, stuff my life to overfilled and overindulged. It leaves me feeling somewhat shameful, pathetic, desperate, weak, and icky.

I don't stuff myself out of sincere lack or need like the chipmunk. I stuff myself out of anxiety and dreams for the way I *hope* to live instead of the way I'm living now. I stuff and stuff and stuff because of the erroneous fear that I will never have enough and that maybe I am simply not enough. I stuff my life out of fear I will fail, I'm on the wrong path, or the path I took—my life—won't matter. The carrot of enough always is j-j-j-just out of reach.

> I stuff because of the erroneous fear that I will never have enough and that maybe I am simply not enough.

When I worked in an ad agency, we used to joke that we convinced people to buy things they didn't need, with money they didn't have, to impress people they didn't know. I know better, yet I still fall prey to the more-more-more mentality.

There are lots of books out now about minimalism—reducing your possessions and living in the freedom of less. They reflect the truth of Scripture: "Godliness with contentment is great gain. For we brought nothing into the world, and we can take nothing out of it. But if we have food and clothing, we will be content with that" (1 Timothy 6:6-8).

My husband grew up with parents who served in ministry and lived by faith. They had no savings account and sometimes didn't know how they would buy food or pay the bills. Yet God always provided. They lived in contentment, and their home was filled with laughter, visitors, and peace. My husband says he always felt rich.

I grew up on the same street as the governor's mansion for the state of Wisconsin. Yet, I always felt that we were poor compared to our neighbors whose homes were filled with Oriental rugs and who took lavish skiing vacations to Colorado. Their children went to exclusive camps and wore monogrammed clothing. My comparison-riddled perspective skewed my reality. I wanted monogrammed sweaters. I wanted expensive camping experiences. And there was never enough stuff I could grasp that could satiate my yawning hunger for more. I had everything I needed, but like Eve in Eden, my heart longed for what I didn't have. It is so easy to confuse need with greed.

Jesus warned us about this kind of avarice, "Beware! Guard against every kind of greed. Life is not measured by how much you own" (Luke 12:15 NLT). In the midst of an economy that only grows through consumerism, this sounds like a foreign language. We can't quite make the connection.

It is so easy to confuse need with greed.

When we overstuff ourselves with the needless debris of life, we are saying, "I live in discontentment. I live haunted by lack. I live in fear that God won't provide. I live in the belief that all this will bring me more peace and joy than what He promises." Ironic, isn't it, that those minimalist books all talk about how shedding our lives of things not only frees up physical space in our homes but also frees up psychic and emotional space as well. Our brains are free from worrying about insuring, dusting, decluttering, organizing, and stuffing all the stuff. A reduction in our stuff makes for a richer and more expansive life. It brings freedom to travel, pursue other interests, invite people over, serve others, and welcome fellowship.

I felt this freedom the time I took 20 boxes of books to Goodwill and carloads of unused knickknacks to our local senior center. I can only imagine how great it would feel to unstuff all our closets and the garage.

Unfortunately, it usually takes a due date or catastrophic event to cause us to want to unload it all in a hurry. Like moving or cancer.

The chipmunk, when threatened or handled roughly, will suddenly disgorge all the contents from his cheek pouches that he has so carefully stuffed full. When we had to move out of our home within ten days, all the items that I thought I would use someday or would sell at a good price suddenly ended up in a heap on the front lawn as we got close to the arrival time for the moving van. I went from, "I'd like to sell this couch for $300," to, "Please, just take it off our hands. And would you like accent pillows with that?"

When my mother was diagnosed with pancreatic cancer, a frantic unloading of many beautiful—but now deemed superfluous—items took place. Quite a few large, silver-plated serving dishes, extra sets of china, Lladro figurines, souvenirs from trips, assortments of curated rocks and fossils, collections of antique Bakelite bangles, tons of craft supplies, and Italian leather purses formed just a few of the mountains of accumulation from 80-plus years of living and two different residences. She couldn't unload it fast enough. Where she was going, none of this was needed. All she was taking with her was her character, which is all any of us take past the portals of this life.

So how do we end up with lives stuffed full of character as opposed to just stuff? Unload the superfluous. Unload the things. Unsubscribe from all the emails offering you sales and deals. Stuff your calendar with dates full of experiences and trips with loved ones, meetings with old friends, and opportunities to serve others. Stuff your calendar with opportunities to be used by God. Stuff your life with moments of eternal value.

In Acts 13:36 it is recorded that King David "had served God's purpose in his own generation." That is the ultimate epitaph you want. That God used you, in your generation, for His purposes. That is what character is made of. That has eternal value. That's what Rick Warren calls the purpose driven life. That's what I call the right stuff.

Exploring Further

1. In what areas of your life do you have too much or tend to overstuff?
2. How does it make you feel when you encounter your own stashes, piles, or moments of stuffing?
3. If you had to leave the house in 30 minutes because of an approaching fire, what would you really need to grab? What would you take in one carload?
4. Read Luke 12:15. How can you apply this verse to your life? What does advertising and the world tell us?

5

Wind

The old Colonial-style windows rattled on the windowsills, and the trees outside clawed the house as they swayed back and forth in the wind. The telephone wires were swooping up and down in a macabre double Dutch jump rope routine. We didn't have a barometer, but the slightly green cast to the sky and the eerie moaning outside told my mother all she needed to know—tornadoes were near, and we had to get down to the basement.

I loved the wild and windy weather—even tornadoes—that came every year to our Midwest town. It meant that we would spend the night in the basement together as a family on couches, watching old home movies of grandparents and family vacations while stuffing ourselves on endless bowls of popcorn. Maybe because none of the surrounding neighborhoods suffered catastrophic home damage, I never had the quaking fear that others with firsthand experience have endured. Instead, it was as if the weatherman had told our county, "Party in the basement tonight!" So we gathered with our poodle, food, and movies and enjoyed lots of laughter. What's not to love?

The fun continued in the morning if the wind was still up. Instead of sleeping in, on windy mornings I jumped out of bed because the wind had whipped up the lake across the street into huge, crested waves. Windy days meant screaming with my friends as we tried to jump over the waves and bodysurf them. It meant flying kites with ease. It meant holding a huge umbrella like Mary Poppins and seeing if we really could travel just a bit, thanks to the wind.

I see this same joy and excitement when I watch windsurfers harness the wind at Ho'okipa Beach, Maui. Their sails and boards leap out of the water and ride the air like stunt pilots. Even the arthritic guys in their seventies come out of the water with a grin.

And my brother's father-in-law, Lon, gets a beatific smile when he talks about the adrenaline rush of iceboating across a frozen lake. I haven't joined him yet, but I get the impression it's like being in an open Maserati hurtling over the bumpy ice while your face ages ten years thanks to the icy winds slapping you in the face at 50 miles an hour. It sounds exhilarating in a teeth-rattling, terrifying way.

As a gardener, I wasn't so thrilled with the daily afternoon wind that always toppled my delphiniums and gladiolas when we lived in the Silicon Valley. I had to learn the art of staking my plants so they could withstand the afternoon blow coming from the East Bay. To my girlfriends from Texas, the wind is a constant nuisance. They have perfected the art of using industrial-strength hairspray as armor protection for their coiffures. My hilarious friend Jodie offered me a chance to try her Aqua Net while we were primping in a restroom. She held out the tall can to me with the promise, "Honey, this will stop Big Bird in flight!"

Where does wind come from? For many years, I thought wind was a result of storms. If it wasn't stormy but windy where I was standing, then I thought a storm was coming—or at least a change in the weather was imminent. This reasoning is partly true: Wind is a result of temperature change.

To be more precise, wind is about the differences in temperature between different locations. The sun hits all the nooks and crannies of our earth at different angles and intensities due to the time of year. Also, because of mountains, open plains, oceans, and all the varied terrain, some places are warmer than others. So now you have pockets—some with warm air and some with cold air.

Like the steam from your cup of coffee, warm air (or high pressure) rises. When this happens on the earth, it leaves a vacancy for cooler, denser, low-pressure air to move in. But the wind doesn't come from the cooler air moving in. Imagine you're sitting in an air-conditioned car on a blasting hot day, and then you turn the car off. Soon, the cool air dissipates and it becomes unbearably hot. The converse is true in cold climates. You might freeze to death if you sit in your car without the heat on winter nights. In both of these situations, diffusion is happening. Meaning, the hot and the cold try to even out. So while the warm air has risen and the cooler air has moved in, the warm air, seeking equilibrium, then swoops down into the areas of cooler air. This is where the wind comes in. And the greater the difference in temperature, the faster the wind moves.

Although we know how wind is caused, we still can't see it, create it, control it, or stop it. The best we can do is harness it. And if you've ever flown over the water in a sailboat with the spinnaker nearly bursting with wind, you know how exhilarating that can be. But as far as controlling it? This is the domain of the One who wrote the laws of physics. And wind in God's hands can bring blessings and abundance or terror and misery. Scripture is full of poetic pictures about the wind.

> When he thunders, the waters in the heavens roar;
> he makes clouds rise from the ends of the earth.

> He sends lightning with the rain
>> and brings out the wind from his storehouses
>> (Jeremiah 10:13).

> On the wicked he will rain
>> fiery coals and burning sulfur;
>> a scorching wind will be their lot (Psalm 11:6).

When Jesus walked among us, the disciples were completely stunned when He demonstrated power over the weather. While they knew He could heal the sick and had wise words to share, controlling the forces of nature was on a totally different scale:

> The disciples went and woke him, saying, "Lord save us! We're going to drown!" He replied, "You of little faith, why are you so afraid?" Then he got up and rebuked the winds and the waves, and it was completely calm. The men were amazed and asked, "What kind of man is this? Even the winds and the waves obey him!" (Matthew 8:25-27).

Jesus not only controlled the wind, He used the wind as a metaphor to teach about the spirit. When the temple priest Nicodemus came to Him secretly in the night to inquire about who He really was, Jesus said,

> Very truly I tell you, no one can enter the kingdom of God unless they are born of water and the Spirit. Flesh gives birth to flesh, but the Spirit gives birth to spirit. You should not be surprised at my saying, "You must be born again." The wind blows wherever it pleases. You hear its sound, but you cannot tell where it comes from or where it is going. So it is with everyone born of the Spirit (John 3:5-8).

Here Jesus reminds us that we can hear the wind, but we don't know where it comes from or where it is going. Sure, our weather

technology can say, "It's coming from the north." But is that precisely
Fairbanks, Alaska? Or over the Bering Sea? And exactly where on the
planet will that puff of wind die out? We don't know. All we know is
that we can hear it and see its effects.

The account of the coming of the Holy Spirit in the book of Acts
is another example of this.

> On the day of Pentecost all the believers were meeting
> together in one place. Suddenly, there was a sound from
> heaven like the roaring of a mighty windstorm, and it filled
> the house where they were sitting. Then, what looked like
> flames or tongues of fire appeared and settled on each of
> them. And everyone present was filled with the Holy Spirit
> and began speaking in other languages, as the Holy Spirit
> gave them this ability (Acts 2:1-4 NLT).

Before this, Jesus had promised them that the Holy Spirit would
come. He didn't say when or how, but He did tell them to "wait for
the gift my Father promised" and instructed them to stay in Jerusalem until it happened (Acts 1:4). He knew that they would be trem-
bling, fearful people without this infilling power that would change
them into confident, dynamic speakers and miracle workers who
could stand up to the might of the Roman Empire.

These verses make people nervous. Some churches teach that the
Spirit-empowered, miraculous acts the disciples took part in died
with the early church. Other churches believe that if you don't speak
in unfamiliar languages, you don't have the Holy Spirit. Maybe we
need not be so eager to box up the wind with our limited understanding. Our Western minds are uncomfortable with things we cannot
explain or control. And as much as we have sequenced our DNA
and sent space stations into orbit, we think that if we can't wrap our
minds around something completely and put a tidy label on it, it

must not be true. But in the spiritual realm, there is much that doesn't conform to our expectations.

I had been a Christian for just a few years when I first met someone who had come back from the mission field in Africa. I didn't know this man, but others in my circle did. We were at a wedding, standing outside milling around in a group before the ceremony started. I overheard this guy, Rick, answering questions about his time in Africa. Clearly, I could tell by the reactions of some in the group, they didn't like what they were hearing.

Intrigued, I moved closer. "It's incredible!" Rick was saying. "The blind are seeing and the lame are really walking!" Many in the group had shuffled away, saying they didn't want to miss the ceremony, but I lingered. Rick went on to talk about events and circumstances in villages where he had been. To his surprise and in spite of his preconceived notions about theology and the way God moves, he was a witness to the movement of the Holy Spirit and the healing power of Jesus's name. It didn't matter what he thought about how things ought to work in God's kingdom. It didn't matter what his theology was. What mattered was the Spirit was moving, with or without him. The wind blows wherever it pleases.

Years later, I was in a completely different church setting (the kind that looks wary when miracles are mentioned) when I heard another woman's account of what she experienced overseas. Suzanne wasn't a missionary; she was just in a group of Christian travelers.

"We came to this village, and they asked us, 'Are you Christians?' We said yes, and they said, 'Oh good. We will get the sick now.' We looked at each other in shock, surprise, and frankly, a lot of discomfort. They lined up the sick in the village and said, 'You can pray now, and we can be healed, right?' We didn't know what to say. None of us had ever been in this situation before. And we didn't have much faith. But with our little bit of faith we hesitantly started placing hands on people and praying for them. To this day, I'm still in a little bit of shock over what happened. It was so surreal and out of our control. It wasn't about what we said or did. It was all about the power of Jesus's name. We prayed for those people, and they were healed. Right before our eyes."

Suzanne didn't speak in other languages, she didn't have her theology lined up, and she certainly hadn't come from a large event where people were on stage pushing people down "in the Spirit." She was just obedient and humbly prayed. And when the Spirit comes, He blows down defenses, doubt, and disbelief.

This is why I am bemused by false representations of this in the media. Because they are drawn to power (and to be honest, who among us isn't?), preachers and teachers get onstage and whip the congregation into a frenzy to "get their miracle." Their stagecraft and tactics are mesmerizing and believable by a gullible crowd desperate for blessings. It's almost as if the order of service reads, *Wednesday night at seven o'clock, cue the Holy Spirit!*

When the Spirit comes, He blows down defenses, doubt, and disbelief.

But can we really cue the power of God's Holy Spirit this way? By getting ourselves worked up into a lather? And is this the only way to "get your touch" from the Holy One who commands the wind and waves? I think the real thing is far more impressive than any staged show. I think there's a better way to heat up the temperature, make a difference, and get the winds blowing in power and authority.

The Hebridean islands off the northwest coast of Scotland are a remote, wild, and woolly place. They consist of islands like Lewis, Harris (as in Harris tweed), and Skye, to name a few. The islands are battered by bitter North Atlantic weather, and the people are resilient, salty, and not easily impressed. But two elderly sisters in their eighties had soft hearts. Peggy Smith (who was blind) and her sister Christine took it to heart in 1949 to pray for their community. The reports talk about the youth in the area being mainly concerned with drinking and partying. There was also a concern that most people were not taking the Sabbath as a day of rest seriously. (My word, look at us today!) Compared to our current time, it sounds like typical teenagers and pretty quaint. But that doesn't mean it didn't concern God. So these old, arthritic sisters got on their knees and prayed from 10:00 p.m. to 2:00 a.m. two nights a week.

To make a long story short, the Spirit of God fell on that community. People who had never darkened the doors of a church felt compelled at all hours of the night to get up and go to the small church. It was packed at three o'clock in the morning! Those who couldn't get in and were out in the fields or walking along the road were overcome by the presence of God. When people could squeeze into the church, services would last several hours. The Spirit of God was so strong that people felt the presence of God all over the island. Those who never even made it to church felt the power of the Holy Spirit. They didn't have to say special prayers or promise certain behavior or speak in a different language. Most of them had no theology, correct or incorrect. But they had the power of God. The bars were boarded up, lives were changed, and people went around the world as missionaries from this awakening.

Duncan Campbell, the minister who was called to preach as it broke out, is careful to give God all the glory and at the time reported, "I did not bring revival to Lewis. I thank God for the privilege of being there…but God moved in the parish of Barvas before I ever set foot in the island." He knew that it was God's work, not his. He said, "The Spirit of God was moving in such a way that I couldn't preach. I just stood and gazed upon the wondrous movings of God."[1] The powerful wind began blowing, and he just rigged up some sails to help others in their journey.

There's a lot of hot air blowing around politics and in the media these days. And throughout history, people have jostled for power. But authentic, life-changing power comes from the One who can still the wind. All He's looking for are some faithful souls who will take prayer seriously and call upon Him with humble hearts. Our prayers matter; they make a difference. And as we join with others in prayer, we cause a temperature shift in the heavenlies. And then the wind will start blowing. Wherever it pleases.

Exploring Further

1. What has been your reaction to a windy day in the past? Do you have a specific memory?

2. Have you ever met anyone who has witnessed or been a part of the moving of the Holy Spirit like Rick, Suzanne, or Reverend Campbell?

3. What do you think of their accounts? Do they make you doubtful, envious, nervous, or something else?

4. When Jesus tells Nicodemus "You must be born again," why did He also then start talking about the wind?

6

Compass

At least the moon is out, I thought to myself, peering at the inky, black water. There were six of us going on this dive, and it was my first time doing a night dive. The boat bobbed in the chilly waters of Port Phillip Bay, Australia, and I tried to act as if it was no big deal. I was a collegiate All-American swimmer. I had done dozens of scuba dives in these waters. This was just another one. Except it was night. And very, very dark underwater.

Our instructor reminded us about watching our gauges for air consumption and making sure both our "torches" (flashlights) were in working order. In potentially dangerous situations, the rule is, *One is none. Two is one.* Meaning, if one of your items is lost or not working, you've got nothing. You'll need a backup. We had backup torches, secondary regulators to breathe with, and the buddy system. The goal of this dive was to complete navigation exercises with a compass for our rescue-level diving certificate course. I was going to be using my new compass I had purchased while visiting home a few weeks ago.

"Let's go, mates!" the instructor said as he heaved himself backward off the gunwales of the boat. We all followed him and flung ourselves backward, splashing onto the surface and gurgling down to the nighttime depths.

Crabs scuttled away from the beam of our flashlights as we descended to the ocean floor. A small trickle of icy water entered my wetsuit and coursed down the back of my neck. I shivered. Fish darted by, and I tried not to be nervous about the fact that I couldn't see further than the beam of our lights. What was out there? Should I be watching for anything? Do sharks sleep at night? But nobody else seemed concerned, and I had a job to do, so I turned my attention to my gauges.

I was supposed to be the compass reader in my group of three. Another person was reading the map on waterproof paper. We followed the instructions precisely. After 30 seconds of finning, I pointed west. Then after a while, north. Then one person started disagreeing and gesticulating that my directions were off. He pointed to his compass—which showed a different reading than mine. I shook my head violently. This was a new compass, and it worked perfectly. They were wrong! They acquiesced to my American confidence and, after 15 minutes of following our instructions, we surfaced together. We blinked stupidly at the shore, which shouldn't have been so far away. We turned and saw our boat, way too far away as well. We looked at each other.

I spit out my regulator, completely confused. Brian, an Australian who wasn't shy about making fun of Americans, was more pointed. "You Yanks! You think you know everything. We are completely off course!"

"But this compass is brand new!" I said, "I just bought it! It's not my fault!"

Brian grinned. "And what hemisphere did you buy your fancy new compass in, sweetheart?" His broad, Queensland accent dripped with sarcasm.

I started to say, "The norther—" but I stopped midsentence. The truth dawned in my brain as my mouth formed a perfect *O*. I had bought this compass in California, in the *Northern Hemisphere,* and Australia, where I was living, was in the Southern Hemisphere! Duh!

Compasses are designed to work with the earth's magnetic field, not with a physical "pole" stuck in the Arctic somewhere. And the earth's magnetic field is composed of several fields, which are all layered on top of each other and interact with each other. They are the Earth's conducting, fluid outer core, magnetized rocks in the Earth's crust, fields generated outside the Earth by electric currents flowing in the ionosphere and magnetosphere, electric currents flowing in the Earth's crust (usually induced by varying external magnetic fields), and ocean currents.

For a compass to work properly, its needle must be free to rotate and align with the magnetic field. The difference between compasses designed to work in the Northern and Southern Hemispheres is simply the location of the "balance," a weight placed on the needle to ensure it remains in a horizontal plane and hence free to rotate. In the Northern Hemisphere, the magnetic field dips down into the earth so the compass needle has a weight on the south end of the needle to keep the needle in the horizontal plane. In the Southern Hemisphere, the weight needs to be on the north end of the needle. If you did not change the weight, the needle would not rotate freely, and hence would not work properly.[1]

So, while my compass was new, it wasn't designed to work in the Southern Hemisphere. It worked *sort of*; it pointed in the general direction, but it wasn't accurate and didn't get me to the right destination. Although I was enthusiastically following it with good intentions, all that energy was wasted. It got me off course so I missed my target. For this exercise, it was a minor inconvenience and a lesson in geophysics. No harm done. But trusting unreliable guides in life can have major consequences. It can result in disastrous results that can last a lifetime.

I met James when he was a quiet, intelligent, and somewhat shy ten-year-old. Years later when he had entered high school, he decided to jump into all that he had missed while living in a sheltered environment overseas: popularity, girls, partying.

He believed his friends at the party when they said, "It doesn't matter if you just inhale a little of this smoke. It's not like you're injecting it into your veins or anything. It's just a fun party drug!" And so began several years of heroin addiction that completely derailed his life.

Some of us have the erroneous notion that heroin use is rare because *who would actually inject a needle into a vein?* But today, that is not necessary. You can smoke it or snort it. And shockingly, heroin can be cheaper than alcohol or marijuana, which is why its popularity has exploded across our country.

The myth or false advice is, "You won't get addicted if you don't inject it." The truth is, any form of it floods the opiate receptors in your brain and will cause cravings that last years—if not a lifetime. It's not so much a moral issue (who of us hasn't made a dumb decision?) as a chemical/biological issue. The one exposure changes your brain so that you are now chemically altered. And countries that treat it as such see more success in treatment centers than the knee-jerk shame, blame, and prosecute approach.

James has lost friends, been in and out of recovery, and seen years of his life swallowed up to this addiction. Not to mention the enormous toll his addiction has taken on his family. He's lucky—he hasn't lost his life like more and more people have as this epidemic sweeps our country. And today, he's holding down a job but has to take a daily dose of medication to curb his chemical cravings for heroin. It's a life sentence that could have been avoided by not following the directions of so-called friends.

Thousands of Americans lost their life savings listening to bad investment advisers who promised to make them rich. I've had friends accept the direction of paid counselors and then give up way too soon on their marriages. They are now wishing they had a partner and are competing for attention with women 20 years younger.

My hackles rise when I walk into a public place such as the auto dealership's waiting room, and I see people glued to the TV screen where talking heads pour out bad advice. They hang onto the words of these "experts" as if they hold the key to success, happiness, and fulfillment in life. It's like those old newsreels of thousands of people riveted to Adolf Hitler's words. Mesmerizing for sure, but accurate? Truthful? Great guidance? Hardly. But the world is full of "experts" looking for "sheeple" to follow their advice.

Sometimes it's our own family members.

The first time I participated in a Bible study, I made the comment, "God helps those who help themselves." The leader, Carol, turned to me with a soft smile and asked in her Texan drawl, "Where'd y'all git that?" I thought for a moment, *Where did I get that?* "I think it was my dad," I said.

Carol answered, "I'm sure your father is a wonderful person, but honey, that's not in the Bible." It wasn't? All these years I had taken that phrase as gospel, and yet it wasn't biblical. (It was from Benjamin Franklin, actually.) I was relieved. I never liked the thought that my work and effort had to be deemed worthy before God would help me. I prefer Jesus's offer, "Come to me, all of you who are weary and carry heavy burdens, and I will give you rest" (Matthew 11:28 NLT).

As Christians, we know where to go for life's direction. But we don't always turn to it. We (okay, I'll just admit it, *I*) often go first to friends, online, the refrigerator, the stash of dark chocolate, and all sorts of self-medicating activities before submitting our plans and desires to Jesus. We think our ways will get us what we want, and we're not so sure about liking what God wants for us. We prefer our own compass—even wobbly and not quite accurate—rather than the one the Bible offers, and this is faulty thinking.

> We know where to go for life's direction.
> But we don't always turn to it.

We want a meaningful life, and we spend our time on meaningless, online activities. We want purpose and direction, and we follow guides whose only purpose is to make money off of us. We want peace, and we fret about missing out. It's all backwards and upside down.

I'm notoriously bad at determining directions. If my husband is unsure of which way to turn while out driving, he'll ask me, "What do you think?" I'll respond, "Everything in my gut says to turn right." Then he turns left. Because we both know I have opposite direction disorder. I'm joking. It's not a *disorder*, but it is freaky how upside down and convoluted my sense of direction is.

One time, when I first got a phone with map apps, it was telling me to go a certain way. I looked at the horizon, the sun setting in the west, and thought, "Okay, I *know* the sun sets in the west, I know a better way. This app is wrong." And, of course, I ended up lost. I treated the app as if it were making suggestions as opposed to having more reliable, concrete information than I did.

The GPS system that smartphones use was first developed by the US military for its own use but now is used by all of us. They work by finding radio signals from a network of GPS satellites. Once a device has located several satellites, it can figure out your position by triangulating from the satellites. In other words, Big Brother is watching and has a literal "bird's-eye view" of your path. It doesn't rely on intuition or feeling. It's scientifically accurate.

How totally laughable of me to ignore its instructions. How completely wrongheaded of me to think my internal compass and intuition work better.

Peter said to Jesus, "To whom shall we go? You have the words of eternal life" (John 6:68). We know this in our heads, but our hearts and feelings lead us astray. I don't recall Jesus ever asking anyone how they *felt* about the truth He offered. "So, Peter, does this deal sound good to you? How do you *feel* about it?" said Jesus. Never.

How do you *feel* about it?" said Jesus. Never.

The truth is the truth whether or not we feel good about it or like it. We can pretend that gravity doesn't apply to us, but we'll suffer the consequences. The Christian walk is never about letting our feelings drive us. It's about letting His faithfulness guide us. This is the opposite of what we hear all the time. "Listen to your heart" or, "Your gut will tell you." That method of direction can change dramatically depending on hormones and what we ate last night.

The Christian walk is never about letting our feelings drive us. It's about letting His faithfulness guide us.

The psalmist writes, "Your word is a lamp to guide my feet and a light for my path" (Psalm 119:105 NLT). The Word of God shows us where we stand and where we are going. It matters not what our feelings or gut says about it. And while it won't show you the path 20 years from now, it's faithful and accurate for today and every day. And that's a guidance positioning system that will work in daytime or nighttime and in any hemisphere. Forever.

Exploring Further

1. Have you ever become totally, completely lost?
2. How did you feel? If you were with someone else, how did they react? Was there blame?
3. Whose advice have you listened to that was totally wrong? Did you know at the time that you were following a false guide?
4. Who or what in your life is a trusted source of wisdom? Where do you go first when you need advice?

7

Falconry

Through our misty windshield, we caught brief glimpses of the top of the seven-hundred-year-old castle as the fog shrouded its bulk. The road wound around beautifully landscaped acreage as we drove closer. Ground mist swirled around the bends in the street and played hide-and-seek with the treetops and shrubs. Our family was going to try falconry at a castle in Scotland, and it felt like we were driving back to the Middle Ages.

Technically, falconry is the ancient art of hunting wild quarry in its natural environment with a trained bird of prey. Practically, all I knew about it was that scary-fast predator birds could come and land on your arm at will. Romantically, it felt as if we could step back through the mists of time by participating in this ancient sport.

Most of us associate falconry with medieval stories of knights, castles, and hunting parties. Although it has been romanticized and popularized in European history and fiction, its origins were most likely in the Middle East. Earliest accounts referencing falconry date back to around 2000 BC. And scholars think it was introduced to Europe around AD 400 when the Huns invaded from the East. It was a popular sport and status symbol among the nobility of medieval Europe, the Middle East, and the Mongolian Empire. And falconry doesn't mean just falcons. Although peregrine falcons are the fastest animals on the planet, hawks, owls, and even sometimes eagles are involved in the sport. Falconry reached its peak around the 1600s, but fell out of favor with the introduction of firearms.

Today, it's experiencing a resurgence in popularity. And I have persuaded my reluctant 11-year-old to give it a try. He's not that into nature, but I keep encouraging exploration. I read him all the nature-related books I could when he was little. I read him the Newbery Medal book, *Rascal,* about a pet raccoon. I had him read one of my favorites at his age, *My Side of the Mountain,* about a boy who goes to live in a tree in the forest. Still, it takes some cajoling to get him to take a walk on the wild side. Thanks to a medieval faire we went to at another castle where they demonstrated falconry, he decided this was something he'd like to try.

We pulled up to the falconry center, and I was immediately charmed. Out in front, a collection of birds calmly sat on individual perches: hawks, tiny owls, falcons, and other birds of prey I can't quite put a name to. A slight brunette with a porcelain face sprinkled with fetching freckles greeted us with a soft, lilting Scottish accent. She looked like she could have been an older friend of the Duchess of Cambridge and I was instantly captivated. She assured us that our son would indeed love this experience.

She fitted him with a huge, sturdy leather glove with a protective gauntlet running nearly up to his elbow. Then she selected a calm barn owl for him to get to know. We walked out onto the great sward of emerald-green lawn that skirted the castle, and I felt like we were on a movie set. The castle's turrets soared high above us, peeking out over the mist. Flying from the top of the turret was the blue

Scottish flag with its white *X* snapping smartly in the breeze. To me, it felt impossibly romantic, beautiful, and serene—almost as if we had stepped back in time.

Our teacher talked about the owl and what it is interested in (food) and what it is not interested in (petting—it annoys them). We learned to respect the owl's preferences, and she encouraged my son to hold out his arm confidently for the first landing. Thanks to a bit of raw chicken, our barn owl flew from his perch 50 yards away and landed deftly on my son's outstretched arm. Huge smile. He did this for a while, and despite his parents oohing, aahing, and taking endless pictures and videos, I could tell he was *dead chuffed* as the Brits say. Quite proud of himself.

We walked back to the building where they house more owls—the mews. There was a giant, great gray owl. And we got to spread the feathers apart and see their massive ear openings, which are about the size of a quarter. No wonder they can find prey much more easily by sound rather than sight. We also saw a ginormous and gorgeous bird that looked familiar. It was a Siberian (or Eurasian) Eagle Owl, and was the granddaughter of Draco Malfoy's owl in the Harry Potter movies. She was the biggest bird in the aviary, with formidable, cruel talons, and we kept our distance. We held and cooed over a tiny little one that was appropriately from the family of Little Owls. It was all so fascinating and too short. We decided to come back again.

The next day we were scheduled to go on a hawk walk—a special time set aside with an instructor to walk in fields and lightly forested areas with a hawk. Our teacher this time was a fascinating creature. Fiona had purple and aqua hair. Over this, she wore a pink crocheted cloche hat. Large, white, cat-eye glasses over heavily made-up eyes

completed the look. I was dubious. Is this the look of a serious fal-
coner? Shouldn't she be wearing a more English country, quilted field
jacket look? Perhaps a pair of sturdy wellies? But I needn't have worried. Fiona demonstrated she was more than capable. She was full of
interesting tidbits of information, and she knew the answer to every
question we had.

For our hawk walk, a Harris's hawk was chosen. Fiona explained
that most would-be falconers start with a red-tailed hawk because
they are a good beginning bird due to their nature. But theirs was
busy elsewhere. We have both kinds of these hawks screeching overhead where I live in California, and I was curious—why is a red-
tailed hawk preferred over a Harris's hawk? One would think a hawk
is a hawk, but no. Turns out it is best to start with a red-tailed hawk.
They are easier to train and have an easier disposition. But the Harris's
hawk is smarter than the others. They can be trickier to work with.
They also have a mind of their own and can be coy about returning
if they don't feel like it.

We walked along our trail, my son's outstretched arm ready to
receive his hawk in the back-and-forth détente of working with wild
creatures. When he wanted the hawk to fly to him, a morsel of raw
rabbit or chicken was placed on his glove. Even if we couldn't see
where the hawk was in the dark mystery of the forest, he knew where
we were. And he knew when food was offered. Eventually, our hawk
became disinterested in our routine.

"He's fed up," Fiona said.

"Oh! What are we doing wrong?" I asked. "Was my son's arm not
high enough? Did he not like the food?"

"No," she laughed. "It means the hawk is not motivated anymore
because he's full of food. He doesn't care—that's *fed up*." Ah. We nodded sagely.

With the hawk peacefully perched on my son's arm, we headed

back to the little building and visited with other birds. "Would you like to try this one?" she asked, pointing to the massive Eagle Owl we had avoided yesterday. At over two feet tall, she appeared solemn, menacing, and mysterious. She faced us in that eerie, knowing way of owls, seemingly measuring us up. Her hooded, golden eyes slowly blinked. The tufts of feathers, looking like horns, fluttered lightly above her head. I remembered what we were told about Eagle Owls the other day. They can take down foxes, lambs, and baby deer, as well as other surprisingly large prey. I was about to answer for my son (like a good helicopter parent) with an "Oh no, she's much too big and scary," when I heard his reply—quick and firm—"Yes!"

I spun around and stared at my usually tentative boy. I wanted to say, "Who are you, and what have you done with my son?" But I thought better about harshing his happy.

Fiona smiled, "It will be fine. She's not as scary as she looks." She then belied that comment by pulling on an even larger, thicker protective glove. The kind you could feed into a wood chipper without much damage. I eyed the owl's two-inch talons, the grip strength that could subdue a large animal, and gulped. Fiona carried the bird out onto the expansive, sweeping lawn and placed him on my son's matchstick arm.

"Is she heavy?" I asked.

"Not really," Jack said. "Definitely heavier than the other birds, but lighter than you'd think." Fiona explained that despite her large size, our owl was actually only about nine pounds. She flapped her wings to settle herself, and we jumped back. Her wingspan was startling—six feet across—and she completely dwarfed and hid our son in the process.

"Aren't you nervous?" I asked. My husband kicked my shoe in the nonverbal message of, *Shut up, don't put ideas in his head.*

"No," he replied with a slight smile. "She's cool."

Eagle Owls are the epitome of cool. They are spread across the European continent from Portugal and Scandinavia in the west all the way to the farthest points of China and the Korean peninsula in the east. They can thrive in coniferous forests and live near deserts. Unlike other large birds, an owl's flight is silent. So they are the ultimate in stealth hunters. And, of course, there are those massive talons with a grip ten times that of a man's—about five hundred pounds per square inch. That's plenty of strength to snap the spine of its prey, plus a hooked beak that can rip and tear creatures apart. Cool.

We were so enamored with these amazing birds and the idea of taking part in a sport that harkens back to the Middle Ages that we talked about how we could do falconry back home in California. "It would be great to find a place like this and try it out for a bit," I told my son. I started to think about all the huge, open space around our neighborhood and the plethora of rabbits and critters. We could dabble in falconry in California! We have plenty of red-tailed hawks. I began babbling about all these thoughts as I do when stoked about something new. This would be great! I had it all figured out! Not so fast, Artemis.

According to our instructor, however, the laws are different in the US than in the UK. You can't just walk up to a falconry center, slip on a glove, and let raptors land on your arm. The rules are much more stringent.

In the United States, you have to get a federal and state falconry license (for us that means through the California Department of Fish and Wildlife). To get this license, you have to pass a written test. Subjects covered will be biology, training, and veterinary care of raptors. And you must score at least 80 percent. Then, you have to find a sponsor to train you. This would be a two-year apprenticeship. Next, you have to build a mews—the proper housing for birds—and add all the equipment. With all that in front of you, you'd have to be *exceedingly keen*, as my British friends would say.

"You know," Fiona said, pushing her white, cat-eye glasses up her nose, "it takes quite a bit of commitment to do this." So what sort of commitment are we talking about, I wondered?

Raptors should be flown at least three days a week and for three hours at a time. That's a minimum. And red-tailed hawks live around 25 years. So those who take on falconry need to evaluate their commitment level. It's not like if things don't work out, you can just turn in your pet to the humane society. You are in a serious relationship that takes an enormous amount of care, patience, and time commitment. Although I'd like to believe differently about myself, to be honest, I knew I didn't have that kind of commitment in me. I knew I probably couldn't follow through on that level.

Commitment seems so old fashioned and quaint these days. We like flexibility, options, waiting until the last minute to bind ourselves to any invitation or event. In our FOMO (fear of missing out), we view commitment as a no-no. God forbid we should miss out if something better comes along. But in some circumstances, it's imperative to commit. Those who pursue excellence in their field—from athletes to scientists—know that commitment is the only way to reap the deeper rewards and benefits. Dallying about won't deliver. It's critical to count the cost and decide whether or not we will be all in. At times, it can feel risky and cliff-jumping scary. But paradoxically, I see a deeper fulfillment in the lives of people who close off other options and give their lives up in service and commitment to a longer-term view.

Robertson McQuilkin knows something about commitment. He was a popular president of a college when his wife, Muriel, developed early Alzheimer's disease in her fifties. At first, he arranged for a home companion to be there during the day when he went to work.

In a magazine interview he said:

> As soon as I left, she would take out after me. With me, she was content; without me, she was distressed, sometimes terror stricken. The walk to school is a mile round trip. She would make that trip as many as ten times a day. Sometimes at night, when I helped her undress, I found bloody feet. When I told our family doctor, he choked up. "Such love," he said simply. Then, after a moment, "I have a theory that the characteristics developed across the years come out at times like these." I wish I loved God like that— desperate to be near him at all times. Thus she teaches me, day by day.[1]

When it became clear that Muriel was highly agitated when he wasn't around and needed full-time help, Robertson stepped down from his job. He was eight years shy of retirement. He was at the peak of his game. The college was thriving. He was a sought-after speaker. Most people encouraged him to hire full-time help. After all, she had Alzheimer's; she wouldn't know if he was there or not. But he said, "I'll know." He states:

> When the time came, the decision was firm. It took no great calculation. It was a matter of integrity. Had I not promised, 42 years before, "in sickness and in health... till death do us part"?[2]

Entering into commitments can bring out the best in us. When there is no escape hatch, when it's inconvenient, when there is no applauding audience, and the way feels desperate and lonely, commitment reveals our character and opens up the path to true, Christlike service. It is here we enter into the kinship of the suffering.

After my 25 years of marriage, I can in no way compare my path to Professor McQuilkin's. But there definitely have been seasons where I wondered, "How long, O Lord?" There have been times where I've felt like smacking myself in the forehead with the comment, "What was I thinking?" Through years of infertility, job loss, financial setbacks, and deaths in the family, it is not always wedded bliss. And my husband would say the same is true for him. There were periods of drought, suffering, and irritation. But there was also warmth, hilarity, and passion. And the longer we are married and weather the ups and downs of a committed relationship, the sweeter the rewards.

> Commitment reveals our character and opens up the path to true, Christlike service. It is here we enter into the kinship of the suffering.

Although we may waver in commitment at times, God never does. His commitment to us is eternal and constant, despite what you've done or are going to do. I take great comfort in the fact that when God called David a "man after [His] own heart," He said this knowing that David would commit adultery and then lie about it and have the woman's husband killed in a cover-up. Not exactly on par with stealing candy! God saw all this coming in the future, and still He called David a man after His own heart. I savor that. Because it means no matter what I do, God sees my heart. His love isn't based on behavior. He cares about my longings and my failings, and yet His commitment to me doesn't waver or falter. Philippians 1:6 says, "And I am certain that God, who began the good work within you, will continue his work until it is finally finished on the day when Christ Jesus returns" (NLT).

Jamie Ivey described what God's commitment toward us looks

like in her book *If You Only Knew*. Despite struggling with partying, drinking, and repeated pregnancies with accompanying miscarriages, she scrabbled her way toward God, only to discover He was always there, loving her. She writes:

> God knew all the days of my life before I was even born, and He still chose to love me and pursue me. This is true for those of you who are stumbling your way toward Jesus as well. God knew how you would turn your back on Him, and He still chose to love you. God knew how you would harm your marriage, perhaps even destroy it, with one poor choice, and He still chose to love you. God knew you would struggle to accept your body so much that it would lead you to purge food from your system daily, and He still chose to love you. God knew you would drink so heavily that you would make choices that hurt those around you, and He still chose to love you. God knew you would have that abortion, and He still chose to love you. God *loves* you.[3]

God says, "I have loved you with an everlasting love; I have drawn you with unfailing kindness" (Jeremiah 31:3). This is a long-term commitment that can withstand whatever you're going through. No matter how many times you fail.

Jesus's parable about the wayward son coming home to his father after squandering his life in wild, self-indulgent living really moves me. Because here we see God *running*. God runs toward us even when we mess up! Show me any other god who does that. As Jamie Ivey would say, "Jesus is better." His commitment to us is better than any other deal out there.

God runs toward us even when we mess up! Show me
any other god who does that.

Commitment creates an undergirding of trust. I wouldn't love and trust my husband as much as I do today without the 25 years of commitment that have passed between us. There can be a rare beauty and fellowship with Christ that can only be entered into through service and commitment.

Falconry, marriage, and much of life's commitments are not for the faint of heart. We will flail and fail often. But when we rely on God's commitment to us, when we lay hold of His promise of constant love, our guilt falls away, we are infused with new strength, and our lives can take wing and soar.

Exploring Further

1. Is there something you've wanted to try but were afraid of the commitment involved?
2. What situations currently in your life require a long-term commitment?
3. When have you been tempted to bail out?
4. Which of the stories or examples in this chapter can you most relate to?

8

Tick

G et out of here!" shouted Jim, turning his face away as the nurse
entered his hospital room. This was after he had thrown a few
choice, vicious names her way. The family members winced and
looked at the nurse with shocked, embarrassed faces.

"Honestly, this isn't like him at all!" said his granddaughter with
tears in her eyes.

"He's really a very godly man," said his wife, resting her hand
lightly on the nurse's forearm.

"That's okay," said the nurse, "I've heard and seen it all before.
Believe me."

Still, it was stunning to the family members gathered around him.
Here was a man who professed to be a Christ follower and had led
Bible studies. Here was a man who had spoken to hundreds about
his friendship with Jesus during his life. Here was a man who was
utterly changed and different from the laughing husband and grandfather so many loved. Who was he really? Which was the real version
of him? The former congenial, gracious host and warm Christian? Or
the angry, swearing, embittered husk festering on the hospital bed?

What caused this transition from proclaiming God's goodness,
witnessing to employees, and enjoying warm relationships to an

angry, hostile, and profane person? It wasn't Alzheimer's. It was a very tiny seed with devastating consequences. Much like a tick.

Most of us think ticks are not a big deal. And if you love the outdoors, you don't want to let such a little thing stop you from enjoying the glories of creation. I've had several ticks on my body, and I didn't give them much thought. Sure, they were pretty gross with their heads stuck down under my skin. But putting a match to their backside or suffocating them with Vaseline always made them pop out their heads so I could get rid of them pronto. And when I thought about Lyme disease, I told myself, "Well, that's easy to prevent—or just get rid of the ticks once they've found you." But now I realize it's not that simple.

Adult ticks are easy to spot. They are about the size of an eraser on the end of a pencil. After coming indoors, you brush off your clothes and then strip down to buck naked and make sure none have crawled under your clothes. (And check all those crevices.) Toss clothes into the dryer on hot for 15 minutes to kill any. If you find a tick, there are lots of ways to get rid of them. But what chills me to the bone is realizing the danger of the teeny, tiny ticks you can't see. The ones you don't know have bitten you.

According to the Global Lyme Alliance, the most dangerous tick to be bitten by is one at the nymph stage. They are the size of a poppy seed. And like all ticks, their saliva has a numbing agent so you can't feel it when they bite. Nor do they always give the telltale "bull's-eye" rash that indicates you've been bitten. Many people never get that rash. These tiny, unfelt bites by nymphs are responsible for the majority of Lyme disease cases. And just what is Lyme disease?

At the end stages, Lyme disease can look like Parkinson's, Lou Gehrig's (ALS), and multiple sclerosis (MS). Meaning, neurological and muscular problems that can have you shaking, twitching, experiencing seizures, and wheelchair bound. Eventually, death awaits.

Pretty serious stuff. But let's back up a bit. What does it look like *before* you get to that stage?

For the victims of Lyme disease, their symptoms can start with seemingly innocuous flu-like symptoms: fever, headache, fatigue, aching joints, and chills. Other symptoms can involve the heart, vision, or hearing. The various displays of Lyme (also known as the "Great Imitator") have baffled doctors into incorrectly assuming it's fibromyalgia, lupus, chronic fatigue syndrome, arthritis, ALS, Parkinson's, and a host of other diseases and ailments. Also, one tick can carry several diseases that work to create a confusing havoc of symptoms.

Amazon has a chilling documentary about Lyme disease called "Under Our Skin." This documentary follows the lives of several sufferers who have spent years chasing down doctors and suffering from this disease. To watch these formerly vibrant, sports-loving adults reduced to semiparalyzed, incapacitated victims is heartbreaking. Such a host of misery from such a tiny little insect. But the good news is, you can take steps to prevent it.

For Lyme disease avoidance, dress appropriately. This means closed-toe shoes, pants that are tucked into your socks, long-sleeve shirts. When you're outside in brush, tall grass, gardens, or mulch, be aware (even near the beach) that danger lurks there. Use insect repellents like DEET, and realize that pets can bring ticks indoors too.

We can take proactive steps to avoid tiny ticks and the Lyme disease they carry. But how can we prevent the scourges of the soul? How can we guard against those seemingly small, insignificant moments that burrow under our skin and infect our hearts and our faith, and ravage our lives as happened to Jim?

I've had many situations where I've not only acknowledged the seed taking hold, I've been reluctant to deal with it—pull it out—at least spiritually. For the man who unjustly fired me from one of my jobs? I shocked my husband when I spit out, "I want to nail a dead cat to his door." My rage and fury were a savory taste of revenge in my mouth. And I *so* wanted to savor it. I knew what I was supposed to do—forgive. And I also knew I couldn't wait for the feelings. I would never naturally feel warm and forgiving toward that man. To me, he was loathsome. But I could act forgiving and say the words in prayer and wait, in expectancy, for my feelings to follow. For some people who have suffered atrociously at the hands of others, this can take years. Some can get over things in an instant. There is no recipe or formula for your path. You just have to be willing, as opposed to waiting until you feel like it.

> Forgiveness is more about being *willing*
> than *waiting for* the feelings.

Before Jesus went to the cross, He certainly wasn't feeling, "Hey, it's all good. This will end well, and wow, the glory afterward will be just awesome!" He was terrorized and terrified. Sweating and agonizing, He begged God to "take this cup from me." Sometimes, even though it doesn't make sense to us, God's holiest and right answer to our pleas is "no." How we respond to our "nos" can determine whether we will end up like Jim in a hospital bed, swearing at everyone, or as a wholesome being leaving behind a legacy of love.

> Sometimes, even though it doesn't
> make sense to us, God's holiest and
> right answer to our pleas is "no."

Maybe you could call Jim's seed that rooted *dashed expectations.* Or *disappointment.* The feelings we have when life doesn't turn out the way we planned. Of course, all of us encounter life's struggles, where events don't play out the way we had hoped. Sometimes it's huge things—like a loved one dying or a spouse leaving. Sometimes it's smaller things. Our marriage has recurring problems. Our job is demanding. We never got the kind of house we wanted. Or our kids didn't turn out the way we had hoped. Those little disappointments, or seeds, if left untended, fester and grow deep in our hearts. They grow into a sturdy weed that reveals itself when all our defenses are down. The Bible calls it bitterness.

Jim had a carefully tended list of grievances he "endured" over the years. His only son had died in Iraq, while his best friend's son had come home. His daughters hadn't taken up his business and had chosen other careers for themselves. He never got to move into the kind of neighborhood he felt he ought to after all his hard years of work. These and other grievances ate at him and fed the weed. It grew deep roots into his soul.

Outwardly, Jim could be the life of the party. He was kind and funny to all. He praised God's name. But when he had too much wine or was tired, or the frustrations of getting older started to take hold, he could snap and say terrible things to his wife. He would blame Emily for all his unhappiness. He complained more than he rejoiced. He blamed more than he apologized. He nurtured and ruminated over his disappointments. Over the years as his health failed, his facade dropped further and further. And now, in this hospital bed, the bitter fruit was there for all to see. Raging, festering, putrid bitterness.

Jim's life was a graphic lesson for his grandkids, children, and the hospital staff. Who wants to end up like that? Who wants their life story to end with poisonous words and warped, blackened memories? Who wants loved ones to recoil in horror? How can we make sure it doesn't happen to us?

Dealing with our disappointments and heartaches is a good start. We can't afford to let those seeds burrow under our skin, take root, and strangle our souls. It's okay to admit to God when we are brokenhearted, furious, or whatever we're feeling. (It's not like He's surprised by this.) First Peter 5:7 says, "Cast all your anxiety on him because he cares for you." We are not fooling God or ourselves when we put up the facade that we're okay while we fester inside over perceived injustices. And PS: God doesn't owe us anything. He doesn't owe us prosperity, a spouse, health, a home, a family, or even citizenship anywhere. Thanks to our daily, unavoidable habit of sin, we deserve death. The kind of agonizing death Jesus died nailed to a rough beam of wood. So anything positive, happy, lovely, or good that you encounter in life is a bonus.

In fact, I know of no better repellent to disappointments, injustices, and burrowing seeds of bitterness that this: gratitude. It sounds galling in light of our suffering, of course. But the more we thank God for all the little things, such as the ability to hear the laughter of a friend, the smell of brewing coffee on a cold morning, an event to look forward to, or just fresh, clean sheets, the more we overcome the pain. The more we focus on whatever is lovely, true, and of good report, the better we root out and destroy the seeds of bitterness. We may not be able to choose what happens to us. But we can choose how we respond.

> We may not be able to choose what happens to us. But we can choose how we respond.

Just like we have to hunt for and get rid of ticks, no matter how small, we will get the same benefit if we hunt down our corrosive attitudes and beliefs. If we don't get rid of them, if we don't prevent them from burrowing under our skin, they will take root inside and choke the life out of us. And that's a wasted life, which can really tick you off.

Exploring Further

1. Have you ever suffered unjustly at the hands of others? How have you responded to that?
2. How did it make you feel toward them? Toward God?
3. Do you know anyone who has struggled with bitterness? Have you?
4. Read Romans 5:6-11. How does this make you feel about what you think you deserve in life?

9

Campfire

The backpack dug into my shoulder blades as we trudged along the trail in Sequoia and Kings Canyon National Park. After the fourth mile, 45 pounds starts to feel a lot more like 110. At least it was dry. That's probably the number one thing I love about outdoor activity in the West. No humidity, no mosquitoes. Thus, I am not cursing under my breath, slapping at bugs with sweat pouring down my face as I would be in the Midwest. Unfortunately, I don't glow like a lady; I gush fluids. But not here, not on this hike. Steve, the group leader for the ten of us friends, assured us that the campsite was worth the effort. We had six more miles to go.

I sure hoped Steve knew where he was going. The so-called signs (small wooden signposts with faded, obscure directions) weren't all that clear to me. I put my head down and followed the feet in front of me. The backpack seemed to get heavier with every mile. Finally, as the sun was starting to disappear behind mountain peaks, we reached our site. Close by was a sapphire blue lake, twinkling an invitation. We all dumped our packs, scurried behind bushes to put on our swimsuits, and jumped in. *Bliss.*

Later that night after setting up tents and cooking dinner, we gathered around the campfire. In this remote spot, there were no city lights, no nighttime glow to dim the stars. Flames leaped up eagerly in the clear mountain air, and we felt enfolded by the soaring redwoods surrounding us. There was nothing to be heard but the crackle of our fire and the murmuring of our voices. As we huddled together and gazed into our communal fire, we traded life stories. Things we had done, things we had left undone and felt regret over. Like sojourners for centuries have done before us, we shared stories that we had never told anyone else. The fire seemed to call forth connection and kinship that couldn't happen in other settings. And for this reason, I love congregating around a fire.

While traveling in Scotland and Shetland, I've been charmed by peat fires. Chunks of dense earth—or peat—were carved out of the ground from peat bogs, dried out in the sun, and burned in hearths. This gave off a dank, musty scent like what you would imagine burning earth would smell like. I liked it. In New Mexico, I was enchanted by the aromatic scent of burning piñon wood. This wood is native to the area, and the smell is utterly different from anything else you can imagine. The Native Americans burned it as incense since it is so fragrant. Apple wood has a lovely fruity smell and burns with a satisfying snap, crackle, pop. But all those fires were in fireplaces. More captivating to me are the outside fires we encircle with friends.

Vacations, campouts, beach gatherings, or outdoor fall parties are great occasions to gather around the fire. Like moths to a flame, we are attracted to the primeval lure of the communal blaze. Around the fire, we slow down, put our feet up, and take a breather. We share stories, hopes, laughter, and unzip our souls. It seems easier to talk while staring at the flames as opposed to bluntly beholding another's eyes for fear of judgment or misunderstanding. The fire is a safe focal point to which we can offer up our tales, give laughter, and present ideas. Those actions—offer, give, present—sound like a sacrifice.

And indeed they are. We give of ourselves, we offer up our stories, our embarrassing foibles, we present our real selves and sacrifice our pride—barriers to being present in the circle of connection. And what we receive in return is the kinship of community.

Community is the invisible vitality vitamin that researchers are just now discovering. In many studies on why certain people live so long and so well (Okinawans in Japan, Sardinians on the Mediterranean), the power of community has emerged as just as valuable as diet and exercise. These groups ate vastly different diets. The Japanese had pickled foods, fish, and a high sodium diet. The Sardinians had lots of cheese, vegetables, and some meat. What they had in common was a strong community.

I've often wondered how my father-in-law lived to be nearly 90. He was technically obese. He enjoyed a rich diet of butter, cream, meats, and homemade pies. He walked a little bit into his seventies, but then stopped because of arthritis. He didn't do much, but he had much. He had a large community from years of being a beloved pastor. And this community adored him. People who had moved away would come to visit and enjoy his hospitality. I believe he was buoyed up with love and kinship and didn't feel despair even when living with one faltering kidney toward the end of his life. Community supported and loved him.

For our investment in health, many of us are quick to jump on the ultimate healthy eating plans. Paleo! Probiotics! Vegan! Mediterranean! Or we try to pick the ultimate exercise regime for fitness. Spinning! Aerobics! Yoga! Weights! But we don't give much thought to the power of community. For robust long-term health, this may be our best bet.

The people of Frome, England, witnessed how the power of community could change lives. In 2013, Dr. Helen Kingston launched The Compassionate Frome project because she kept encountering patients who were frustrated by the medical world treating them like a collection of symptoms instead of a human who happened to have some health issues. Kingston partnered with government health agencies to set up programs and community groups to facilitate her ideas. Namely, help people not be so isolated.

Illness tends to reduce socialization opportunities, and we hunker down. This used to mean hunkering down with family. But now that families are spread far and wide, this just means isolation and loneliness. Then it sets up a cycle: Get ill, retreat, get isolated, get lonely, and get even iller because you are isolated. The more isolated we are, the more the cytokine chemicals get released into our bodies. These act as messengers in the immune system and cause inflammation, change our behavior (withdrawal), and then contribute to depression.

To combat this cycle, Kingston set up "health connectors" to help patients manage their care and find the support they needed. This could mean handling housing issues, joining choirs, lunch clubs, men's tinkering shops, or exercise groups. The hope was to break the cycle of illness, isolation, and depression. It worked. While the surrounding county had an increase of emergency room visits, in the town of Frome, they went down by 17 percent. But this isn't surprising. Studies show that those with strong social relationships have better health and a 50 percent lower chance of death.

Community also has a quelling effect on addiction. Johann Hari has a fascinating TED Talk[1] where he illuminates the power of community on experiments with rats. If you put a rat in a cage with two water sources, one plain and one laced with cocaine or heroin, the rat will quickly prefer the drug and kill himself in a short amount of time. But if you put that rat in a cage with climbing structures, entertainments, and most of all, lots of other rats, almost no rats take the drugged water. When they are not isolated, devoid of community, the rats don't need or want the drug. Hari went on to demonstrate how the same structures of community and support made a significant difference in returning Vietnam veterans who had been heroin users. Those who had strong, supportive community around them experienced little recidivism.

While we may not be addicted to drugs, I think we can safely say that we are all in some measure addicted to entertainment, comparison, and material possessions. Hari states in his book *Lost Connections: Uncovering the Real Causes of Depression—and Unexpected Solutions*, "What you really need are connections. But what you are *told* you need, in our culture, is stuff and a superior status, and in the gap between those two signals—from yourself and from society—depression and anxiety will grow as your real needs go unmet."[2]

Community and connection are the antidotes for anxiety, isolation, and depression. A caring community cultivates contentedness. This is reflected in the Hebrews passage where it states: "Let us think of ways to motivate one another to acts of love and good works. And let us not neglect our meeting together, as some people do, but encourage one another, especially now that the day of his return is drawing near" (Hebrews 10:24-25 NLT).

First-century Jewish believers in Jesus had no centralized place to gather. The temple was now closed to them, and in Jerusalem they were suffering persecution and disconnection and a diaspora. So they scattered and had to meet up wherever they could—homes, fields, whatever worked. But gather they did. In our twenty-first century, we have the erroneous notion that we can experience the fullness of the Christian life by going solo. Sure, we will have epic, contemplative moments while surveying a beautiful view, or a quiet thrill while reading a compelling book, but organic growth is best fostered in a group gathering of like-minded souls.

A caring community cultivates contentedness.

In a group, you learn from others' experiences. In a group, you can get encouragement that you are not crazy—or that your type of crazy is okay. In a group, you can learn how to study the Scriptures and apply them with power to your life. In a group, you can experience laughter, tears, insight, and camaraderie. In the supportive setting of a small group, spiritual growth happens.

Popular author, speaker, and pastor John Ortberg says, "Community is what you were created for. It is God's desire for your life. It is the one indispensable condition for human flourishing."[3]

When our family decided to stop driving 20 miles to the church that we were married in and find something closer to home, we had a new perspective on what mattered. We didn't know that many people in our town. We were homeschooling our only son, and although he was involved in scouting and sports, we still didn't have much of a sense of community. So the church we chose wasn't about the most amazing teaching or rapturous worship; it was about relationships. The people were warm and welcoming, and we kept bumping into members at the local store, the bank, the hiking trails, and the local restaurants. We chose our church mostly because of the opportunity of community it offered.

Community means relationships. And relationships are where fellowship and friendship happen. Jesus wasn't concerned with the beauty of the buildings of worship. We never read about Him being impressed with any church leaders—whether teaching or worship leaders. He was all about hanging out with the people. Scruffy, outcasts, or leaders, He gave them equal attention and time. And He encouraged drop-ins.

When I was living in Australia, I was astounded at how often people would think nothing of dropping by without any notice. (At times it caused this clutter queen quite a bit of anxiety.) But I also found it charming. It showed me that in this society, togetherness was more important than my to-do list.

Although we are supposedly more connected than ever through various social groups online, the reality is, it's vaporous. As a woman I know pointed out, "There's no actual person to run to the store for you. None of these online 'friends' are available to just drop by without many weeks' notice. Everyone is so busy." So how do we find actual human connections when we are running our kids to soccer, running errands, and running just to stay in place? How can we shift our priorities to facilitate gathering together more?

Consider the fire pit.

Landscape designers know that the fire pit has replaced the pool, koi pond, and expensive landscaping as the number one desired feature in the backyard. Why are these such a hit? Because they are casual. They extend gathering and living spaces. And probably unconsciously, they fill that gut need we have to gather together. Since Eden we have been congregating together for warmth, stories, and companionship. A fire pit makes this happen.

Depending on where you live, your local laws will determine whether or not you can legally burn things. Now that studies have been done about air quality and how burning wood contributes to air pollution and necessitates "spare the air" days, there are fewer areas where it's okay to burn wood. With the massive forest fires that have ravaged communities out West, the idea of an outdoor wood-based fire is maybe not the best approach.

Since Eden we have been congregating together for warmth, stories, and companionship.

There are more options, such as gas fires. I used to think these were icky and fake. I love the smell of wood, plus the crackle and snap of wood fires. They smell like fall, football, earth, and everything cozy to me. So what's the appeal of a gas fire?

For one thing, less mess. There are no ashes to take care of. Also, you don't need to have advanced Boy Scout skills to start it. Turn on the gas, light the flame. Done. It lights perfectly every time. And, you don't need to worry about getting to the store because you are running out of wood. Of course, those who live out in the country are chuckling at that. Buy wood? Well, for those of us in the suburbs and cities, yes. We have to buy it, and often we don't have the room or the necessity to store a cord of wood. Our nation's plentiful natural gas, as opposed to electricity, is cheap by comparison. We have vast stores of it under the crust of our nation's boundaries.

You can get your gas fire pit in ground or above ground. It can be part of a table or a simple cement block structure. The fire can leap out of metal logs, ceramic logs, modern chips of fire glass, or my favorite—lava rocks. My sister has a huge fire pit with a center pile of lava rocks. What makes this so great is that the rocks warm up and then deliver residual heat. And gas fires aren't known for heat. They are pretty, clean, and convenient, but they don't give off heat like a wood fire. The lava rocks do.

I also appreciate a fire pit that has a place to put your feet. My sister's has a sloped edge of cement, so it's easy to prop your feet up and toast your tootsies. I've seen some with a surrounding rough stone ledge, which also can accommodate the feet-up position. I'm not so keen on tables around them because unless you are drinking hot chocolate, who wants a warm drink? But others find them modern and love them.

Whatever style you choose, the main point of a fire feature is to encourage gathering together. And because of its casual nature, no fussy canapés required. Chips, cheese, and crackers are just fine. S'mores are even better. This makes it easy and approachable for neighbors to come over and makes it fun to entertain outside.

If you want community, it's not so much about your home decor, the best music track, or fabulous food; it's more about being available. Because in the end, we are all just scattered souls needing to huddle close, put down our phones, and share stories. That's the power of community. That's how Jesus built His church.

Exploring Further

1. Have you ever experienced a memorable campfire? Where? Who were you with?
2. What made it so special?
3. Have you ever felt part of a close-knit community? Where and when? What made it feel safe?
4. Have you ever been a part of a faith-based small group? Or been with others who could pray for you? Why or why not?

10

Survival

The mysterious hulk of the submerged fishing boat loomed up in the murky, bluish light as we finned closer. Its blue-and-white paint job was mostly eroded, but it still had a jaunty feel as it sat incongruously on the ocean floor. My dive buddy, Sam, immediately found a way inside the wreck and began exploring the wheelhouse area. I stuck to the outside, peering into the windows and watching the soft corals wave back at me. I turned to watch clown triggerfish and schools of striped jacks cruise by. Sam had moved back outside the wreck and swam off ahead of me. I turned around and headed after Sam's fins, which were rapidly disappearing into the gloom.

But I couldn't move. Something in my equipment had snared on the wreck. I tugged and finned purposely forward. As a strong swimmer at six feet tall and 165 pounds, I could exert significant force if I wanted to swim in a certain direction. But the boat held me fast. I twisted and turned and thought, *Surely my dive buddy will notice I'm missing*. He didn't. *Selfish jerk*, I thought. *He's too caught up in exploring to notice I'm not around.*

Fighting a rising sense of panic and exasperated with Sam's distractibility, I pulled my dive knife out of its sheath strapped to my calf and banged the metal handle against the bottom of my air tank behind my back. *Clang! Clang! Clang!* It was surprising how loud that noise could be so deep underwater. I banged it three more times, sheathed it, and began to take off my equipment. I wasn't going to run through my precious reserves of air while waiting for Sam. It was probably just one of my hoses—maybe the octopus, the secondary breathing regulator—and if I could take everything off and turn around, I could unhook it. I clenched my teeth around the air supply in my mouth and began the process. *No need to freak out*, I told myself. *This is not a big deal, just deal with it, slip your vest back on, and you'll be on your way.* I put all thoughts of danger and how deep underwater I was out of my mind because I knew panic kills. Attitude is everything.

When I'm deep underwater on a scuba dive, I am an actor. I pretend I'm naturally cool and collected. On land, I am a type-A control freak, extremely expressive, and not shy about loudly sharing my opinion. I can easily spin out over not locating papers or someone treating me wrong. But underwater I pretend that nothing bothers me, and I take everything slower than normal. I assume the attitude of a Jedi master. *Hey...what's this now? Hmmmm...let's take it slowly...* It helps that I am at home in the water, but in the back of my mind I know: Those who panic die. I know this from reading many books in my favorite genre.

I have an obsession that my family makes fun of. I refuse to be cowed into shame and submission because I think it might save my life one day. I love books about survival. Fiction is great (*The Jakarta Epidemic; Alas, Babylon; One Minute After*) but nonfiction is even juicier (*The Survivors Club, Deep Survival, The Unthinkable,*

Unbroken, The Hiding Place). These are real stories about real, average people who survived catastrophic accidents and conditions. They have endured plane crashes, being mauled by cougars, being tortured in prisoner-of-war camps, escaping the 9-11 Twin Towers collapse, or hiding from Nazis. Their stories fascinate, awe, and inspire me. Who survives? Who dies? And why?

The first aspect of survival that I noted in all these books was wrapping your mind around the new reality. Many people were frozen and immobile when the Twin Towers fell. Their minds couldn't grasp what was really happening. It was so foreign and so surreal that they couldn't process it. When the unthinkable is happening, the brain has a difficult time sorting it out. Flight attendants are now trained to scream and bark orders at seemingly catatonic passengers to snap them out of their zombielike state and get them moving. In disasters, the brain floods with dopamine, adrenaline, and cortisol to create a chemical stew that gives us the deer-in-the-headlights response.

For example, I read about a plane crash in which a businessman had just read the safety instructions about the plane and noticed where the exits were. (Notice that says *plural* exits—sometimes the one closest to you is blocked.) Once the plane had crash-landed and was filling with smoke and flames, he quickly undid his seat belt, shouted at his shocked companion to do the same, grabbed her hand, and led her toward the exit. As they turned to look back at the other passengers, many were unharmed but frozen in their seats. They were immobilized by incredulity with slack-jawed expressions as smoke filled the cabin. Many of them died.

Usually when people think about survival, their minds conjure up a supermuscular commando type. A guy bristling with weaponry and knowledge of martial arts, endurance in all terrains, a huge survival kit, a commanding presence, and an attitude of "winner takes all."

But when I talked to the mother of a Navy SEAL, she said, "Mostly, it boils down to adaptability. Can you perform at a frigid minus-30 degrees with frostbite or at 103 degrees with steaming humidity? Can you adapt cheerfully and maintain a positive mental attitude when everything is falling apart around you? These are the guys that survive. It's not so much about physical fitness as it is *mental* fitness. The Rambo types who are full of bravado are the first to collapse." It seems attitude is more important than "muscular-tude." Brains over brawn. A cool head prevails in calamity.

Fortunately for me in my diving snafu, Sam finned back to me when I was nearly done with the job of disentangling myself and helped me finish it. But despite my efforts to remain cool, I was close to freaking out. I let him know with my hand signals what I thought about his performance as a dive buddy.

Most of us are not going to have to escape from a burning plane or disentangle ourselves while 80 feet underwater with our air supply running low. We just have to survive everyday life, which has plenty of challenges. The spouse who takes off, the job loss, the scary diagnosis, the rebellious child, and a myriad of other trials test our mettle.

But the lessons from survivors are the same. Along with the skill to accept reality and tamp down panic is the ability to form a plan. Most of the time it's merely doing the next thing. And then the next thing. Sometimes it's as simple as staying awake or holding tight and focusing on not getting tossed out of the life raft. Sometimes it's getting out of bed, showering, and doing the laundry when your loved one has been killed, your child is in intensive care, or you've had a scary diagnosis. Do the next thing, then the next. Take small steps forward, thank God, and celebrate each one.

Elisabeth Elliot is one of my favorite authors and a supreme survivor. Her husband, Jim, was killed by Amazonian Indians with spears when he tried to share the story of Jesus with them. She had a ten-month-old daughter when Jim died, and Elisabeth still went on to live with the tribe, learn their language, and work with them (and forgive the murderers).

> Do the next thing, then the next. Take small steps forward, thank God, and celebrate each one.

Elisabeth was blessed with another marriage, but then that husband lost a long battle with cancer. She married a third time, and it lasted until her death in 2015. She has written honestly about the struggles we all face in surviving and thriving.

She writes,

> Faith, we know perfectly well, is what we need. We've simply got to exercise faith. But how to do that? How do we exercise anything at such a time?
>
> "Pull yourself together!" With what?
>
> "Cheer up!" How?
>
> "Think positively!" But that is a neater trick than we are up to at the moment. We are paralyzed. Fear grips us tightly; grief disables us entirely. We have no heart.
>
> At such a time I have been wonderfully calmed and strengthened by doing some simple duty. Nothing valiant or meritorious or spiritual at all—just something that needed to be done, like a bed to be freshly made or a kitchen floor to be scrubbed…Sometimes it takes everything you have to tackle the job, but it is surprising how strength comes.[1]

Accepting the situation—no matter how unthinkable—and taking action, even in small ways, is the first step to surviving the calam-
ities of life. The injured mountain climber in an icy crevasse needs to
accept that help is not coming and haul his way out with ice ax inch
by inch. The mother of toddlers who has just received the devastating
news that can't be fixed needs to get dinner on the table. The prisoner
in a Nazi death camp with no hope of rescue can decide whether or
not he will give up. Meanwhile, with little movements forward, with
prayer, you make progress. Or sometimes, it's just about not giving
in to despair.

Louis Zamperini, the World War II hero of the book and movie
Unbroken, manifests this firm resolve. He writes in his book *Don't
Give Up, Don't Give In* about his abuse and torture at the hands of his
Japanese captor, "the Bird."

> I had taken the Bird's daily beatings at Omori, and then at
> Naoetsu. I had to. I never complained. I just got knocked
> down, bled, got up, got knocked down, bled, got up. I
> expected it. I wouldn't let it get me down. Sometimes it
> took me two days to recover, but I always had a positive atti-
> tude. Steely, but positive. No way would he break me…I
> wasn't reaching for glory at Naoetsu. I just wouldn't give
> the Bird the satisfaction of destroying my dignity. Don't let
> anyone take yours away, either.[2]

Zamperini went beyond his fierce resolve once the war ended
and ended up not just surviving but thriving. After enduring post-
traumatic stress disorder nightmares, nearly strangling his wife in his
sleep, and alcoholism, he gave his heart to Jesus at a Billy Graham
crusade. He went on to forgive his tormentor and was forever free
from the corrosive thoughts and nightmares that had plagued him
for years.

Over two thousand years ago, Paul the apostle endured ship-wrecks, beatings with rods, being nearly stoned to death, imprisonment, hunger, abuse, and a myriad of other hardships as he went about the Mediterranean sharing the freedom that Jesus had given him and all who trust in His work on the cross. Paul learned that the secret to thriving—not just surviving—is to accept the situation and persevere in Christ. In his letter to the Philippians, Paul writes,

> Yes, everything else is worthless when compared with the infinite value of knowing Christ Jesus my Lord. For his sake I have discarded everything else, counting it all as garbage, so that I could gain Christ and become one with him. I no longer count on my own righteousness through obeying the law; rather, I become righteous through faith in Christ...I don't mean to say that I have already achieved these things or that I have already reached perfection. But I press on to possess that perfection for which Christ Jesus first possessed me. No, dear brothers and sisters, I have not achieved it, but I focus on this one thing: Forgetting the past and looking forward to what lies ahead, I press on to reach the end of the race and receive the heavenly prize for which God, through Christ Jesus, is calling us (Philippians 3:8-9,12-14 NLT).

The secret to thriving—not just surviving—is to accept the situation and persevere in Christ.

The apostle Paul had difficult circumstances and so did the Son of God. So we shouldn't be surprised when hard times come. They probably won't be life-or-death situations. But whether it's a disaster relating to avalanches, addictions, or airplanes, our attitude can be the same as that of Paul, Louis Zamperini, or Elisabeth Elliot. We can accept reality and press on. We can make small plans and take baby steps. With the help of God, we can not only survive, but thrive.

Exploring Further

1. Have you ever felt shocked, immobilized by life events crashing in on you?
2. What helped you take the first steps? Or who helped you?
3. Which of the survival stories can you most relate to? Why?
4. Paul says he "forgets the past." Are there things in the past that you think might be holding you back?

11

Great Horned Owl

Quick! Turn the lights out!" I said as I skulked around from window to window, cautiously peering out around the blinds of each one.

"But why, Mommy?" asked my son, Jack. All he got was a frantic hand waving and a curt, "SHHhhhhhh!"

I couldn't ignore the hooting. It was so penetrating and close. Almost as if we had a pet owl inside the house, and I wanted to find out where this great horned owl was.

Finally, I spotted him, perched on top of the roof that covered part of our driveway. Right near my son's bedroom window. Dang, he was big! I was used to the size of songbirds and red-tailed hawks. But this guy at two feet tall seemed formidable and ginormous. He stopped hooting. I pulled back behind the blinds. I ran to another bedroom where I wouldn't startle him, carefully raised the window, and pressed my face against the screen. I began hooting back into the soft darkness. "Who-who-Hooooo…" He answered! "Who-who-HOO!"

"Who-who-Hooooooooooo!" I again called out in what I believed was an imitation that would have impressed professional ornithologists. Jack stood behind me, bewildered at his bizarre mother hooting out the window.

"What's going on?" boomed a loud voice, shattering the moment. I jerked up, smacking my head on the window. "Ouch!"

My husband was standing in the doorway. Light was spilling in from behind him, and I could see he was frowning in concern at his wife, who was obviously losing her mind, hooting out the window.

I began hooting back into the soft darkness. "Who-who-Hooooo..." He answered! "Who-who-HOO!"

Our owl came by nearly every night, hooting mournfully and soulfully while I read storybooks to our son. I thought he was the coolest thing. So majestic, mysterious, and wild.

I asked our neighbors if they had seen him. Mike, a furnace installer and repairman, nodded and started chuckling at the memory as he pushed back his hair with a beefy, tattooed hand. "I went out there one night and stood in the driveway. He was on that little roof over our driveway, and I was about 15 feet away. I'd never been that close to an owl before. I stared back at him and raised my arms like a bird to see if I would frighten him. That huge bird did the exact same thing and started coming toward me!"

"What did you do?" I asked. I didn't think much of anything could intimidate Mike.

He laughed, "Squealed like a girl and ran inside!"

Owls can be intimidating. With their large size, nearly five-foot wingspan, slow blinks, and ability to turn their heads 180 degrees, they are a world apart from your average chickadee or bluebird. The great horned owl's talons can clench hard enough to break the spine of their prey, and it would take us 28 pounds of pressure to break that grip. And unlike other birds that you can hear flapping as they wing by, their flight is absolutely silent. This is because of the structure of their wings and feathers. You'll never hear them coming.

They travel mostly at night, which just adds to their mystery, and their hearing is astounding. Experiments have shown that owls can locate their prey just by sound, even blindfolded. When they are spotted during the day roosting on a branch, they don't twitter about and chatter. They sit there, stoic, unruffled, and seemingly all-knowing. No wonder they earned the moniker "wise old owl." But what I find totally amazing about owls is the way they get rid of excess parts of their food.

When an owl eats a rabbit, mouse, vole, or small critter, it digests the muscle, fat, skin, and internal organs—and what his body doesn't need or use gets pushed out his "vent" in a milky-white substance. But what about the bones, claws, skull, fur, and feathers he can't digest? These leave via another path.

Unlike most birds that have a crop—a bag-like area that allows birds to store food to be digested later—owls instead have a gizzard. The gizzard uses fluids and gritty substances like sand to help break down the indigestible materials and then trash-compacts them into a neat pellet. This pellet is usually regurgitated a few hours after eating. While it is moist immediately after leaving his body, the pellet (about three to four inches long) quickly dries out. Sometimes if they ate a furry creature, they resemble dry, fluffy cigar ashes. Which is why I didn't recognize them when I first started kicking them aside in our driveway.

I came out one morning to check on the sprinkler system. It wasn't reaching a certain area where I was training a sweet climbing rose to meander up by the side of the house. Before I got to the lawn, I saw what I thought were fat cigar ashes. *How tacky*, I thought. *Can't people smoke in their own driveways? Do they have to use mine?* I kicked them aside and attended to the rosebush.

The next day I went out again. Again I found the chunky remains. People can be such slobs! I grouched and kicked them aside. But this time I noticed that there were hard white bits in the "ashes." Then it dawned on me. These were not cigar ashes. These were fluffy, furry owl pellets full of bones. Cool! I immediately bent down to carefully pick them up. I walked inside with my treasure and showed hubby and son. "Look! Owl pellets! They barf them up when they are done eating. Aren't they cool? We can dissect them! We can discover what kind of animal it was!"

I looked at my son's face. He screwed it up in an expression you would expect if I asked him to smell dog feces. "Ewwwww, Mommy! That's gross!" I looked at my husband for support. "Don't look at me!" he said, backing away with his hands up, "I am not remotely interested in those things; in fact, I don't think you should bring them into the house. They're probably diseased."

"Nonsense!" I replied with an air of cool scientific superiority. "I am going to soak these things in water and see what kind of bones emerge. People do this sort of thing all the time!" I have no trouble with employing the logic of "I don't always know what I'm talking about, but I know I'm right." They both rolled their eyes at their weird housemate.

Soaking the pellets in water did indeed reveal some interesting bits and pieces. I could make out a tiny skull, claws, and other bones among the floating furry bits. Nobody else shared my enthusiasm for my discovery. No matter. I was thoroughly enjoying it. I wondered how such a big chunk could make its way out of their beaks. I wondered if it was uncomfortable unloading such a solid packet.

It made me think about how freeing it would be to sort out all the half-truths, click bait, political messaging, health claims, and spiritual gobbledygook that seep in through our ears and eyes and stew around in our souls every day. How tidy and simple it would be to expel, like an owl, all the useless and indigestible data, fears, and falsehoods that weigh us down. All the social media comparisons that make us feel less than and not enough. Sort it all out like a coin changer or software scrubber and then every night dump out the useless bits in a neat package.

> How tidy and simple it would be to expel, in owl style, all the useless and indigestible data, fears, and falsehoods that weigh us down.

While we can visit Snopes.com for urban legends and rumors and fact check with curated media outlets like the *New York Times*, few realize the plumb line that is already available to us to fact check the swamp of half-truths and spiritual psychobabble so pervasive these days.

Builders don't use a plumb bob much these days, but they've been in use since the Egyptian pyramids—if not longer. A plumb bob is a heavy weight at the end of a string, which creates a plumb line. It helps builders know if they have a wall or doorway straight and absolutely dead centered. Nowadays, builders have moved on to lasers. But as one builder told me, "When the batteries run out on our lasers, you better believe we have a plumb bob in the truck."

When I'm feeling spun around by social media (She is always traveling to fabulous places! Everything he writes ends up on the bestseller lists! Her home is perfect!) and less than, not quite, and just short of a full measure in my walk with God, I have my own plumb bob to help me get centered. It's where people who struggle with shady pasts, frustration with God, and doubts about direction hang out—the Psalms.

When I'm gobsmacked at the success of the crazy, gluttonous, and wicked, I read Psalm 73:1-12 (NLT):

Truly God is good to Israel,
  to those whose hearts are pure.
But as for me, I almost lost my footing.
  My feet were slipping, and I was almost gone.
For I envied the proud
  when I saw them prosper despite their wickedness.
They seem to live such painless lives;
  their bodies are so healthy and strong.
They don't have troubles like other people;
  they're not plagued with problems like everyone else.
They wear pride like a jeweled necklace
  and clothe themselves with cruelty.
These fat cats have everything
  their hearts could ever wish for!
They scoff and speak only evil;
  in their pride they seek to crush others.
They boast against the very heavens,
  and their words strut throughout the earth.
And so the people are dismayed and confused,
  drinking in all their words.
"What does God know?" they ask.
  "Does the Most High even know what's happening?"
Look at these wicked people—
  enjoying a life of ease while their riches multiply.

This writer knows what it feels like to face the folly of Silicon Valley. I can relate to this! And it puts into perspective my own struggles and issues:

Then I realized that my heart was bitter,
  and I was all torn up inside.
I was so foolish and ignorant—
  I must have seemed like a senseless animal to you.

Yet I still belong to you;
    you hold my right hand.
You guide me with your counsel,
    leading me to a glorious destiny.
Whom have I in heaven but you?
    I desire you more than anything on earth.
My health may fail, and my spirit may grow weak,
    but God remains the strength of my heart;
    he is mine forever (Psalm 73:21-26 NLT).

The Psalms are full of plumb lines weighted down with truth. We can get our hearts right and our thoughts straightened out by comparing them to God's truth, not the subjective and relative "truth" the world offers us. The "God helps those who help themselves" kind of twisted theology and patchwork myths from popular sages can really pollute the purity of what God offers us.

> We can get our hearts right and our thoughts straightened out by comparing them to God's truth.

I rarely get sick. I mean the hurl-up-your-breakfast-and-last-night's-dinner kind of sick. I never even got sick during pregnancy. But I clearly remember how incredibly great you can feel after doing so. Before that point, I'm tossing, turning, and trying to quell the churning, sweaty feeling that's threatening to overwhelm me. But once I surrender, wow. I may have a 103-degree fever, but in that moment after, I feel like I can leap a tall building. Relief!

Maybe it's time for me to think about sorting, scrubbing, and disgorging much of what I let slip past my filters every day as "truth." When I start to get that churning feeling in my gut, the less than, not quite, and *if only* feelings, I know it's time. Time to disgorge all that useless garbage the world calls "truth" and realign with God's truth to get relief. Then I'll experience the peace that only God's Word can provide and become truly wise. And that's worth hooting about.

Exploring Further

1. How do you usually feel after reading about your friends' lives online? Do you ever feel envious? Or wish you could enjoy what they are enjoying?
2. What places online do you visit the most? Lifestyle? Home decorating? Fashion? DIY?
3. If you took three days off of all social media, how do you think it would feel?
4. Are there any false ideas/beliefs you have digested that you could get rid of?

12

Stars

John fiddled with and adjusted the knobs and dials on his telescope. He squinted through the lenses while I glanced up and down the dark streets like a rabbit exposed in the middle of the road. Because, in fact, we were in the middle of the road. It was a warm summer evening in Palo Alto, California, and my friend, who was in the astronaut program at NASA, determined that this was the best place to show me the stars.

"Here," he said, "look through here. You can see the constellation of Pleiades. You know, of course, that this constellation is mentioned in the Bible—in the book of Job, where God speaks of His authority and asks, 'Can you bind the chains of the Pleiades?'" (Job 38:31).

I didn't know that, but since we were part of the same Bible study, I felt I should have. I peered through the lenses at the twinkling pinpricks of light, then straightened up and looked at John. "So you're telling me I'm looking at the exact same stars as they were two thousand years ago?" I asked.

John smiled at me indulgently. "Well, technically, longer than two thousand years ago—Job was written before Jesus's time. And the universe is expanding…but yes, the same."

John went on to describe different types of stars—dwarfs, giants, supergiants—and their different luminosities. Their colors can be red, orange, yellow, blue, or white. They have names from antiquity, like Sirius, and crazy-sounding names, like Betelgeuse. Then he described how stars are formed. They start out in a state of clouds and dust and gases. Then a star's own gravity causes it to collapse in on itself, so the center becomes denser and hotter from pressure. Particles start to stick together and then fuse—which becomes the energy source of the star. It "switches on" and begins to shine. The hydrogen atoms fuse and become helium. This nuclear fusion creates the energy that powers every star. He went on to describe how some stars are more massive than our sun, and that they fuse heavier and heavier elements—all the way up to iron—and then have an iron core. At which point they have no more energy from fusion, and over time they collapse in on themselves and end up in a massive supernova explosion.

My brain was collapsing in on itself and about to explode with this tsunami of astrophysics, but I got back on track when he said, "Scientists believe that all the elements in our periodic table were all created inside a star, from the fusion of helium and hydrogen, and then dispersed in the explosion—the Big Bang." Now that was compelling. One massive, energetic, creative moment from which all the building blocks of matter were created. It's fascinating how science and faith can intertwine in lyrical dance.

But all this star talk was a bit too academic for my tastes. While it was impressive and dazzling, I prefer the romance of stars and how they hint at a loving and imaginative Creator. I like to think of His hand scattering the confetti of brilliance across the carpet of sky. I like to ponder God's immensity, artistry, and care for the great and small things He has made. The psalmist said, "When I consider your heavens, the work of your fingers, the moon and the stars, which you have set in place, what is mankind that you are mindful of them, human beings that you care for them? You have made them a little lower than the angels and crowned them with glory and honor" (Psalm 8:3-5). And again the psalmist remarks, "He determines the number of the stars and calls them each by name" (Psalm 147:4).

They may have been formed by gases and nuclear fusion all in a big bang, but that doesn't mean He didn't set the forces in motion, nor does it make them any less enchanting and poetic.

I like to ponder God's immensity, artistry, and care for the great and small things He has made.

It's been said that Tycho Brahe, the brilliant Danish astronomer who built on Copernicus's heliocentric universe and paved the way for astronomers Kepler and Galileo in the 1600s, said, "Those who study the stars have God for a teacher."

Which is basically what Psalm 19:1 says: "The heavens declare the glory of God; the skies proclaim the work of his hands."

Although star creation consists of powerful cycles of elements fusing and growing, exploding in a tug-of-war between gravity and energy, the science begets contemplative wonder and delight. I love the quote by Ralph Waldo Emerson: "If the stars should appear one night in a thousand years, how would men believe and adore, and preserve for many generations the remembrance of the city of God which had been shown!"

From recorded history, the stars have been the object of curiosity, omens, romance, verse, mystery, and delight. Cave paintings in Europe that date back 10,000 years depict their formations. Their varied arrangements—which we sort into constellations such as Orion (the hunter) or the Bear (which includes the Big Dipper)—are usually easily seen, even if you live near a bright, modern city.

In the San Francisco Bay Area, with a population of seven million people and an ever-present ambient light spray, John and I needed a telescope to look past the city glow to find our Pleiades constellation. The best night-sky viewing is done in the absence of light pollution, which is why serious observatories around the world are in remote locations. The darker your surroundings, the more dazzling will be the stars in the sky.

But it's getting harder to find dark places in which we can be dazzled. Although most of us are aware of the plastics filling up our oceans (as well as pollution of other sorts), few realize the light pollution that is filling our nighttime skies. The Dark Sky Initiative and other similar organizations are working to change this. They point out that most of our cities' light litter is from streetlights. That glow you see in the sky surrounding urban areas? That's because the light particles from streetlights are scattered by the atmosphere, which creates the glow across the landscape. This could be greatly mitigated by shielded, downward-facing lights.

But is this really a problem? So what if there's a glow around our lit-up areas? Here's something to think about. Light pollution causes migrating birds to crash into buildings. Just-hatched sea turtles mistake the glow of streetlights for the moon shimmering on the ocean and head inland, where they are crushed by cars. And then there's the waste. Lighting up the nighttime wastes money and fossil fuels. To keep a 100-watt lightbulb turned on for a year takes the equivalent energy output of a half ton of coal. With the switch to more efficient LED lights, cities have gotten even brighter, obliterating the chance to view the night-sky wonders. In fact, scientists from the Light Pollution Science and Technology Institute in Italy say the Milky Way is no longer visible to more than a third of the world's population.

In my teenage years, it drove me crazy that my father was always turning off lights in the house and commenting on how much money we were wasting. I would think, "What's the big deal over a few lightbulbs?" Combined with those of everyone else in the world, it is a big deal. I want my son to be able to see the Milky Way. I want others around the world to experience the glorious display of the evening star show by simply stepping outside, without the need of telescopes.

Years after my experience with John, I didn't need a telescope to be mesmerized by the starry night. I was working in Australia with an ad agency, and we were scouting out locations for a photo shoot in the middle of nowhere—the outback of the Northern Territory, to be exact.

I didn't want to breathe too deeply; it hurt too much. The kiln-like air muffled all desire for movement. There was no cooling sweat to be had as the punishing, arid sun slammed down on the surrounding boulders and our necks. We tried to huddle in the scant shade of a large rock, but even there the temperature was 104 degrees. Usually, I'm quite cranky when I'm overheated, but I was incapable of being irritable in this heat; it just sucked the life force out of me. I looked out across the desiccated landscape and wondered for the hundredth time, *How do people live in this place? Why would they want to live here?*

This place was appropriately named Devils Marbles, and it was about 50 miles from a spit of a town called Tennant Creek, nearly in the center of the Australian outback. The "marbles" are massive, red-granite boulders—some up to 20 feet across—incongruously stacked and balanced in the middle of a flat, arid desert. We were there to shoot a magazine layout for Telecom Australia (now Telstra), depicting that even way out there, back of beyond, there was phone service.

After scouting out the location, we all headed back to the local motel. Our photographer told us we had to be back out there the next day by 4:00 a.m. because he wanted to capture the early-morning dawn against the massive red boulders. So, that next "morning" we staggered to the cars at 3:30. I slumped down in the backseat, trying to catch a few more winks. A short drive later, in the black stillness of the outback, devoid of civilization's lights, we arrived at Devils Marbles. My workmate Dean got out of the car and said, "Wow...wow!" And then, "Get up, Laurie, you have to see this."

"Go away." I didn't like mornings any more than heat, and actually, it was too early to be morning yet. So, no, on both counts.

Dean's shoes softly crunched the dusty gravel as he slowly walked around the car in the dark. "Seriously," he said, "Get up!" He kicked at my shoe dangling over the edge of the seat.

"Awright!" I snapped and pushed myself up off the backseat. I heaved my hardly awake self upright next to the car and glared at Dean. "What?" He looked skyward, and I followed his gaze.

Miles from anywhere and with no ambient light, a deep black, Arabian night sky twinkled with an impossible carpet of diamonds winking back at me. The Milky Way was clearly defined, boldly rending the heavens with its distinguishable swath of billions and billions of tightly clustered lights. The Southern Cross, viewable only in the Southern Hemisphere, blazed in the sky like it does on the crisp blue Australian flag.

I blinked in astonishment. "Ohhhhh," I said. I had never seen stars that clearly. In the absence of lights and civilization's glow, it felt like you could reach out and touch them. They seemed to be benevolently hovering, tantalizingly close and full of mysterious, twinkling wonderment. I understood now why the ancients had spent so much time arranging the stars into constellations and making up stories about them. In the absence of electricity's glow, this enfolding darkness unveiled secrets worthy of such scrutiny and stories.

> I understood now why the ancients had spent so much time arranging the stars into constellations and making up stories about them.

Here's another secret about the stars: The light we see from the stars is not instantaneous. Meaning it has traveled many light-years to get to us. So, as we look at the constellations, we are actually looking back in history. We are seeing light that left those stars light-years ago. (A light-year is 5.88 trillion miles.) When you know how many light-years away a star is, you subtract that number from the current year. When we gaze up at Orion's belt, the star on the far right, Mintaka, is 916 light-years away. So the light we are seeing left that star around AD 1103. Robert Curthose, Duke of Normandy, has returned from the first Crusade, and he invades England in an attempt to take the throne from his brother, Henry I.

The light from the star on the far left of the three on Orion's belt, Alnitak, is 817 light-years away. Therefore, the light we see is from about the year AD 1202. We are looking at light from the time of King John of England. The fourth Crusade is underway, and the Maori have started settling in a place soon to be called New Zealand. And the Big Dipper? The last star in the handle is named Alkaid. Its light left around 1912—the same year the Titanic sank.

Above all else, I love the egalitarianism of stars. The fact that kings, mothers, children, and the homeless are privy to the same view satisfies me. In this world of increasing disparity between rich and poor, as the chasm yawns ever wider, I like it that we all can enjoy front-row seats to God's magnificent light show. Stars are for everybody. Rich or poor, First World or two-thirds world, black or white, we all have the same opportunity to view them. They don't shine any brighter for a world leader or a gang member. The stars remind me of God's love. It's always there, whether or not you can see or feel it, and it doesn't beam down differently for the church leader or the drug user. "The ground is level at the foot of the cross," the old saying goes, which is an egalitarian view of God's grace. There is no high or low standing when we are all standing there.

> The stars remind me of God's love. It's always there, whether or not you can see or feel it, and it doesn't beam down differently for the church leader or the drug user.

The more I know about God's starry masterpiece, the more I want to find dark skies to sit under and ponder it. Now I understand the truth and meaning of John Muir's insight: "When we contemplate the whole globe as one great dewdrop, striped and dotted with continents and islands, flying through space with other stars all singing and shining together as one, the whole universe appears as an infinite storm of beauty."[1]

That night in the Australian outback, while our photographer scrambled around scouting for the best angle before the coming of sunrise, I kept my head back and marveled at the celestial jewels overhead and their infinite storm of beauty. How extraordinary that in a dry and desiccated place named for the devil, I could behold the artistry of the heavens.

Exploring Further

1. When have you had a moment on vacation or away from cities where you saw the stars clearly? What impression did that make?

2. Read Psalm 8. What verses resonate with you the most?

3. What in God's creation fills you with the most awe? Have you ever been in a "dry and desiccated place" and yet still beheld beauty?

4. How does the thought that "the ground is level at the foot of the cross" make you feel about your own situation or about other people?

13

Aroma

I am time-travelling today. I'm seven years old, walking to school along the bumpy sidewalk in our suburban neighborhood. It is uneven because massive oaks and ash trees have lifted up the pavement here and there over the last 75 years before I walked this path. A few houses down the road from ours, right in front of my piano teacher's home, is a bountiful lilac bush. After many long months of Wisconsin winter, the spring season is eager to explode with color and perfume. And this lilac bush is positively summoning me to pause and dillydally along my path. It leans over the fence, alluring me with its luscious fragrance, and I can't resist burying my nose into its cool blossoms and inhaling deeply.

So today, when I smelled the florist's bouquet of lilacs at my sister's house, I was instantly transported to that journey to school when I was a little girl, skipping down the sidewalk.

To smell is to inhabit and inhale history. Of all the senses, smell (and its kissing cousin, taste) has a direct route to emotion and memory in our brain. Our other senses (seeing, hearing, touching) travel through the thalamus in our brain. This is like a gate to our consciousness. Ever notice how when you are reading an article, you miss what someone says to you? That's your thalamus deciding what you are aware of and what you are not. After the thalamus decides what to do with the sensory input, it sends it to other areas of the brain to be processed. But when we smell something, the thalamus doesn't get invited to the party. When the molecules of lilacs are washing over our olfactory receptors, the information bypasses the thalamus and zings right to our limbic system—the area responsible for emotion and memory. It is also the part of our brain that contains our flight or fight responses. This is why, without bidding, an aroma can suddenly take us back in time and jig an immediate emotion.

The briny tang of ocean breezes sends me back to when I first smelled it in high school. We were on a spring field trip, and our buses made the long journey from Wisconsin to Florida. As we came closer to the ocean, we lowered our windows and stuck our heads out like eager, inquisitive dogs, sniffing the unfamiliar sea air.

The unique smell of burning piñon wood reminds me of the time we visited relatives in the Southwest and watched a neon orange and purple sunset. They had a crackling fire of these particular logs welcoming us with its aromatic scent.

When I smell gingersnaps baking, it is Christmastime. I am ten years old and have come in from ice-skating outside. I drop my snow-encrusted mittens, hat, and boots by the back door and enter the warm embrace of the kitchen. The smell of gingersnaps means home, mother, Christmas, and love. My son loves these cookies so much, he wants me to make them year round. But I am hesitant. I don't want to dull or muddy the association I have with that particular scent memory. Nonsensical and silly, but there it is.

Even years after my mother died, I pull out a scarf that had been hers. The scent of her wafts around my closet, and tears spring to my eyes. It's as if she is right there, caressing my neck with love and Arpege perfume.

To smell is to inhabit and inhale history.

Aromas don't always have a good association. For a while after our dog died, rats were attracted to our apple tree. No longer deterred by our feisty bichon, they helped themselves to the apples and then inexplicably died under the house. Until the rodent removal service could get to our home, I burned scented candles. Years later, those same lovely scents trigger a gag reflex in me. They bring back the pungent stink of decaying rodents that I tried to mask. "I smell a rat" has an indelible meaning for me now.

My friend Jennifer had a tough childhood with mercurial, vindictive parents. When she smells packaged chicken potpies, she gets an instant migraine. I asked her about what memory it triggered. She can't remember, but all she smells is pain. When I smell potpie? It's the scent of babysitters and my parents going out to a party.

My friend Sofia is from South America. While I gratefully inhale the pungent, exotic fragrance of tuberose blossoms, to her, they are repellent. They remind her of sad funerals when she was growing up. So scent, combined with experience, gives us the memory stamp our brain recalls.

Happy smells to me are freshly ground coffee beans, summer rain on hot pavement, fresh earth turned over in the spring, just-cut grass, fall leaves burning, popcorn, swimsuits pungent with lake water, eucalyptus trees in heavy fog, bacon on a cold morning, the top of a baby's head, gardenias floating in a bedside bowl, and many other scent markers that speak to me of love and memory.

Gardeners know that certain herbs and plants have terrific scents to perfume the garden and evoke memory. Among my favorites are tuberoses, gardenias, pink jasmine, honeysuckle, orange blossoms,

Oriental lilies, rosemary, thyme, and bay laurel. And recently, rose suppliers have begun reintroducing scent into their breeding programs, which has been lost over the years in pursuit of perfection of form. I always get a kick out of my Dolly Parton rosebush. Its voluptuous blossoms are an intense pink with a knockout fragrance. And even though the ivory rose French Lace is packed with vicious thorns, I love the fragrance. David Austin, an English breeder of old-fashioned roses, produces plants with gorgeous, peony-type blossoms and fabulous fragrance. My favorite is the apricot/pink rose, Abraham Darby.

A scent can not only delight us and send us back in time, it can save our lives. The ability to smell fire, food that has gone bad, or a gas stove that has been left on is integral to living long and prospering.

Aromas can also mete out justice. Bloodhounds are unique among dogs in their sniffing abilities. Their skill at scent tracking is so profound that it is admissible evidence in a court of law. This is due to the fact they have about 300 million scent receptors. That's 40 times the number in humans. And among all breeds of dogs, the bloodhound's olfactory area is the largest percentagewise. This means that smelling an article of clothing from a toddler who is lost creates a detailed "odor image" in the bloodhound's brain. It is more detailed than a photograph for us. Thus, once a bloodhound identifies a trail, he will not be diverted by thousands of other smells that crisscross his path. And he will still be able to pick up that scent days later after many others have walked over it or even if it has rained.

The most famous example of a bloodhound sticking to a trail and delivering justice is a Kentucky bloodhound named Nick Carter. His abilities led to the capture and conviction of more than 600 criminals throughout his career. In one case, Nick was able to follow a scent trail that was over 100 hours (more than three days) old. That record was broken in 1954 when a bloodhound in Oregon got on the trail of a missing family after the police had given up and a week had passed. The dog found them.

Scents can signal whether we are lost or found. In the book of 2 Corinthians, there is this passage that portrays a Roman military triumph:

> But thanks be to God, who always leads us in triumph in Christ, and manifests through us the sweet aroma of the knowledge of Him in every place. For we are a fragrance of Christ to God among those who are being saved and among those who are perishing; to the one an aroma from death to death, to the other an aroma from life to life (2 Corinthians 2:14-16 NASB).

I always found this passage a bit odd, until I understood the history. When the Roman army would defeat an enemy, there would be a grand parade—or triumphant procession. The apostle Paul no doubt had seen or heard of these, which is where his visual illustration came from.

First in the parade lineup would be the vanquished captives in chains, destined for death. Then would come the spoils of war—gold, silver, armor, and statues. Next would be the Roman senators and officials, and after them the general's bodyguards. Following them would be the purple-robed general wearing a laurel wreath, riding on a chariot. He was the focus of the procession. Behind the general would come his adult children and then the conquering soldiers. All along the triumphant procession would be strewn flowers and the smell of incense from burning altars everywhere.

To the conquerors, the aroma of incense would signify victory and celebration. To the captured in chains, it was the smell of death because once the procession had completed its route, the captured were immediately put to death. So Paul is saying in effect that living out our lives as followers of Jesus will cause an aroma to emanate off of us. To one group, it will be repugnant, a smell of loss and death. To another, His victory over sin and death and new life for believers will be the aroma of triumph and being found.

> Living out our lives as followers of Jesus will
> cause an aroma to emanate off of us.

It's bizarre when you see this play out in your own life. In my first job out of college, I was working in San Francisco. A group of us women had gone out to lunch to talk about an upcoming ski trip we were planning. Suddenly, without provocation, one of the women looked at me with a sneer and said, "Are you going to bring any of your goody-goody church ladies along?" I was stunned. I had never discussed my faith life with her, so how could she know I was in a Bible study? And furthermore, among the "church ladies" were survivors of sex addiction, incest, and drug abuse. So not exactly a goody-goody group either. Everyone at the table was openmouthed at her attack until someone else tactfully changed the subject.

For days afterward, I couldn't figure out the *why* of that comment. Why did she say that? Why did it matter to her whether or not I was in a Bible study after work? (Did she think that would affect my skiing?) Why had she felt the need to embarrass and attack me like that?

Later I learned that her grandmother had been murdered in a random shooting while coming home from errands. She was bitter and angry with God for allowing such a horrific event to devastate her family. To her, anything to do with God was a stench in her nostrils. It made sense to me, and I understood that she wasn't angry with me per se, but with whom I represented.

We can't know everyone's background or spiritual journey, so it's pointless to overthink how our aroma affects others. It's between them and God to work out their frustrations and failures. Although we would like to be "the sweet aroma of the knowledge of Him in every place" we can't control others' reactions. But in our conduct we can aim for the response, "I've just been with Jesus" as opposed to, "Dear Jesus! Who have I just been with?"

To be around Jesus was to inhale the fragrance of life in its fullness. Jesus exuded a pleasing aroma when He turned water into wine at a wedding party so the host wouldn't be embarrassed. To His mother, who made the request, and to the host of the party, it was the aroma of compassion. When He called the shunned tax collector Zacchaeus out of the tree and offered to have dinner with him, He was the aroma of inclusion. When He healed the leper, the blind, and the crippled, He was the aroma of mercy. When He cried at the death of Lazarus, He was the aroma of empathy. When He hung out with sinners, He was the aroma of fellowship. When Jesus hung on the cross—beaten, bloodied, and innocent—He was the aroma of love. After the resurrection, when He gave Peter the responsibility to "feed my lambs" despite Peter having denied Him, He was the aroma of forgiveness.

When we follow in Jesus's footsteps and show compassion, inclusion, mercy, empathy, fellowship, love, and forgiveness, we are a "sweet aroma of the knowledge of Him in every place." That fragrance can be so compelling; it draws people and changes lives.

> To be around Jesus was to inhale the
> fragrance of life in its fullness.

Maria Missoni was a nun that my husband, Tom, hired into his start-up in the 1980s. She had been a hospital administrator and was in semiretirement but wanting to work. At first, Tom was dubious. This was a hip start-up company. Was hiring a nun a good idea? Could she really contribute in the frenzied and fierce Silicon Valley culture? But upon the recommendation of others, he hired her. A while later, he discovered that there was practically a line outside her office of people wanting to talk with Maria. Seems she had a steady stream of people who were drawn to her warm and accepting presence, and they felt safe discussing their lives with her. Although it was a secular culture and over a quarter of the employees were PhDs in science, Maria started a thriving Bible study and prayer group. And sweet little Maria was a lot of fun too. At barely five feet tall, she handily beat the pants off 6'2" scientists at Ping-Pong. She was beloved by everyone, and in her presence was the fragrance of love, acceptance, and joy.

We don't have to be a nun or a corporate CEO to make a difference or love people. By welcoming those who feel excluded, or being an empathetic listening ear, a merciful parent, or even a joyful Ping-Pong player, we can exude the fragrance of Christ wherever we are. It will draw hearts closer, open up relationships more quickly, and change lives more powerfully than finger-wagging ever could. Even when people betray us, we can emanate the fragrance of forgiveness. We can spread the beguiling aroma of the kinship of Jesus. The most captivating perfume in the world is the fragrance of Christ.

Even when it doesn't make sense, we can make perfect scents.

> The most captivating perfume in the world
> is the fragrance of Christ.

The disciples didn't think it made sense when the former prostitute took a valuable alabaster jar of perfume and broke it open over Jesus's head. As the valuable nard dripped through His hair, and the scent wafted through the room, they harshly pointed out that it was a stupid waste of resources, and she could have sold that for a year's wages. Jesus had a different reaction.

> "Leave her alone," said Jesus. "Why are you bothering her? She has done a beautiful thing to me. The poor you will always have with you, and you can help them any time you want. But you will not always have me. She did what she could. She poured perfume on my body beforehand to prepare for my burial. Truly I tell you, wherever the gospel is preached throughout the world, what she has done will also be told, in memory of her" (Mark 14:6-9).

When we pour ourselves out as a fragrant offering in love and service to others, we leave a lasting memory of the pleasing aroma of Christ. And that's a scent to die for.

Exploring Further

1. What are some of your favorite scents? What memories or emotions do they trigger?
2. Are there any aromas that you associate with bad memories?
3. Have you ever had anyone react to your "aroma" in a positive or negative way?
4. Maria Missoni spread a loving aroma simply by being joyful and loving. How can you emulate her example? With whom?

14

Fireflies

I t felt as if we were in the midst of *The Legend of Sleepy Hollow*. Washington Irving's home, Sunnyside, quietly loomed over us in the growing August darkness. Its fanciful mishmash of Dutch Colonial, Scottish Gothic, and Tudor revival styles made for a storybook-looking home. It sat serenely along the banks of the Hudson River where distant lights shimmered on the dark surface as the current surreptitiously slipped past. The historic home seemed to hold secrets as it sat hushed in the growing dusk.

Warm evening breezes danced across the lawn and made the fat Japanese paper lanterns sway softly above our tables under the trees. Silverware, finger bowls, and stemmed glassware graced our place settings and glittered up at us from our elegant tables. Our friends had picked a fairy-tale location for their wedding reception. The jazz band was starting up, practicing a few notes and rippling through their scales. It was all so beautiful and surreal; it felt like I was on a movie set. I turned to my husband to remark upon the perfection of this moment when something caught my eye.

Beyond the glow of the party, across the darkening lawn in the wooded border, tiny lights began to glow and diffuse. They rose and fell like a magical fairy accompaniment to our sparkling lights. The breath caught in my throat, and I blinked back tears that threatened to spill over.

"What's wrong?!" asked Tom, alarmed at my sudden change in mood.

"Fireflies!" I said in a whisper. "Look at them!"

It had been a long time since I had been east of the Rocky Mountains in summer. Having lived out West for several years, I hadn't managed to make it home during the summer months. So I hadn't seen any fireflies—or lightning bugs—for years. I had forgotten how magical and mysterious their ballet of light could be. Like earthbound constellations, they rise up in the mystical time between dusk and darkness to twinkle starlight in a bit of suspended heaven that enchants and delights children and adults.

One of the privileges and delights of parenthood is letting your young child stay up later than usual and introducing them to the charm of fireflies. Instead of the nighttime routine of bath, book, and bed, it's a magical moment to watch them witness the wonder of fairy lights out on the lawn.

The first time our son saw them we were visiting my husband's parents in rural Pennsylvania. I had prepared for this occasion with a Mason jar and punched lid. We opened the screen porch door and stepped out into the midsummer night eve. Our three-year-old squealed with excitement and, clapping his hands, ran about trying to catch them. He surprised us by spontaneously shouting a self-made poem for the moment: "Catch them! Catch them! There are ten!" Fireflies bring out the poet and wonder in all of us.

> One of the privileges and delights of parenthood is letting your young child stay up later than usual and introducing them to the charm of fireflies.

There's a reason I hadn't seen any fireflies out West. They love humid environments like forests, marshes, or places near standing water such as rivers and lakes. They need a moist setting to survive, and the West is typically dry. Although there actually *are* a few fireflies in rare places in the West, they don't light up like they do in the East.

Fireflies are not really flies but beetles, members of the winged beetles *Lampyridae* (Greek for "shine"). While there are more than 2000 species of winged beetles, only some have the ability to illuminate. And not all fireflies flash the same color. Some glow a bluish or green tint, and some are orange or yellow. And why do they shine their own little flashlight? For the same reason that birds flash their feathers and frogs croak. To attract a mate. This ability to produce their own light is called bioluminescence.

There are many inhabitants of the ocean that are bioluminescent (jellyfish, fish, octopuses, et al.) and more of them the deeper you go, but fewer on land (glowworms, certain centipedes, and some mushrooms).

Fireflies take one to two years to mature, and they only live as adults for 21 days. So the firefly light show is a short season—and getting more elusive. Due to habitat destruction (outdoor lighting, overmowing of lawns, paving over wild areas), their numbers are declining. They thrive in areas that aren't too carefully maintained, are a little wild, and are devoid of chemicals and bright lights. This doesn't mean you don't mow your lawn, but maybe not so often and leave rough edges or areas to encourage fireflies. And use organic lawn treatments. Once their home is destroyed, fireflies don't move and resettle. They just die out.

In some areas around the world, these interesting creatures thrive and continue to put on unique displays. For a brief eight days every

summer in the Great Smoky Mountains National Park, lucky win-
ners of a lottery draw are treated to a dazzling spectacle. The unique
firefly *Photinus carolinus* delights pilgrims with a rare, synchronous
light pattern. The nighttime forest floor is lit up by an undulating
harmonious flash of light. Instead of the common pattern of one bee-
tle lighting up, pause, and then another in random patterns, this display happens in unison. It is so dramatic and delightful that the park
service has had to limit enthusiasts to a certain number via lottery.
Sightseers are exhorted not to use flashlights or catch the performing
beetles, and to take great care to stay on the paths.

If you miss out on the lottery, there are a few other places around
the world to witness synchronous firefly displays. Malaysia, Thailand,
and the Philippines also have fireflies that light up the night together.
However, these displays are usually high up in trees and have a dis-
tinct, off/on pattern as opposed to the wave pattern on the forest floor
of the Smoky Mountains.

We are mesmerized and attracted to these moments of light in
the gathering darkness. So much so that we will travel to distant
locales to secure a spot to witness these unique flashes of magic. These
glimpses of light, set against the dark backdrop of wild places, stand
out as incongruous and enchanting. Perhaps that's the reason we are
so captivated by them. This is a forest; there should be no light here.
But there is light for those who seek to discover it.

Maybe that's why Ann Voskamp's book *One Thousand Gifts*
has sold over a million copies. Ann's traumatic childhood, which
involved witnessing the death of her sister and having a mother who
was in and out of the psych ward, led her to record moments of light.
One thousand flashes of gifts that she could be grateful for. *Morning
shadows across the old floors, jam piled high on the toast, moonlight on
pillows*... Her simple list of gratefulness, the glints of light in the darkness of her struggles, is a beacon to the rest of us soul-weary sojourners. We can do that. We *need* to do that.

There is light, for those who seek to discover it.

Gregory Boyle is a Jesuit priest who picked the dark corners of Los Angeles to live among the gangs. He is another person shining light into the darkness. He asked the question, "What if we were to invest in gang members, rather than just seek to incarcerate our way out of this problem?"[1] And so while the rest of Los Angeles gave up on the gangbangers, Greg rode his bike into their neighborhoods and sought them out. He believed they could be more and do more with their lives. He shone a light of hope and commitment that drew them and sparked their own lights. When Greg joined his light with others' financial gifts in the community, Homeboy Industries was born. This organization was founded to give gang members job skills, social skills, tattoo removal, and light for their future. They have a drool-worthy bakery with tempting goods made 100 percent from scratch, and they started a solar panel job-training program. Their website states:

> For over 25 years Homeboy has engaged the imagination of more than 120,000 gang members helping them to envision an exit ramp off the "freeway" of violence, addiction and incarceration. Homeboy has become the largest, most comprehensive and most successful gang rehabilitation, and social enterprise organization in the world.[2]

The homeboys work side by side with former archrivals and enemies and learn that joining their lights with others creates a beacon for other gangbangers to emulate. Boyle's example of "no matter what" love is a shining example of how to illuminate a path for those who are trapped.

Jesus said, "You are the light of the world. A town built on a hill cannot be hidden. Neither do people light a lamp and put it under a bowl. Instead they put it on its stand, and it gives light to everyone in the house. In the same way, let your light shine before others, that they may see your good deeds and glorify your Father in heaven" (Matthew 5:14-16).

When I was younger, I didn't like that verse. I mean, I constantly was blowing it. Why would I want anyone to pay attention to my light? I was a horrible example of a Christian. I did my best to keep my light hidden. That way, I could avoid ridicule and embarrassment. I could avoid dragging Jesus's name through the dirt. But what I didn't understand is that God can use my real, sinful self much better than He can a poster child for perfection. Nobody feels at ease around someone who seems to have it all together. Who feels comfortable around that?

The first time I went to my friend Lucinda's house, I had arrived after their midmorning muffin snack. Lucinda has seven kids and homeschools them. So you can imagine the crumbs and disarray under the table. I immediately bent down and began wiping them up with a paper towel. She protested, "Oh, Laurie, you don't have to do that!" I smiled. This just made my day. There was no pretense here, no perfectly decorated home ready for the magazine photo shoot. "You have no idea how much this blesses me," I said. I immediately felt warm, accepted, and needed here. Her lack of pretense opened the door to a genuine, authentic friendship built on shared openness.

We can let our dim, not-so-bright lights shine because when others see our authentic selves, they feel encouraged to let theirs shine as well. I've noticed more and more women sharing stories of abortion, sexual abuse, chemical dependency, and all sorts of struggles from the stage these last few years. What they know is that if we are really going to reach hearts, we have to let our little lights shine, no matter how weak the flame. It's more important to hear, "Me too!" than, "Wow, look at that perfect life!"

When we pretend that our lives are perfect, we don't draw people, we repel them. Nobody likes feeling inferior, less than, or not quite making it. But when we are honest about our struggles, it draws people to be open with us. There is a sense of laying down the burden, exhaling, and fostering acceptance.

We are fallible flames in the hands of a faithful God. It's not about our perfect light, but His. I like what Martin Luther is credited with saying: "I'm just a beggar telling other beggars where to find bread."

We don't have to move to the barrios or stand on a stage to let our light shine. We can just bring someone a listening ear and a loaf of banana bread. Start with what you love. My friend Marta loves to read and wants others to experience that joy. She volunteers with a literacy organization in town to help teach local immigrant children to read. Marta has joined her little light with other instructors so that a whole group of kids who would be left behind are brought into the light. In the midst of life's dark corners, one little light can shine very brightly. But when we join with others with our little lights, we create a luminous, synchronous wave of light that's beautiful to behold and draws people to be a part of it.

> We are fallible flames in the hands of a faithful God.
> It's not about our perfect light, but His.

The news these days is full of people who proclaim to love God but who act abominably. As they express hatred and suspicion for the different, and calloused pride toward the downtrodden, God's love and light gets snuffed out. So even more, we need to step up and shine. I love the approach that Madeline L'Engle describes: "We draw people to Christ not by loudly discrediting what they believe, by telling them how wrong they are and how right we are, but by showing them a light that is so lovely that they want with all their hearts to know the source of it."[3]

That's an enchanting radiance that charms people and draws them near.

Exploring Further

1. Have you ever seen or caught fireflies in a jar? Where were you?
2. Whose life, among your friends, shines a light that draws others?
3. What areas of your life do you feel disqualify you from shining your light?
4. Who in the Bible did God use despite them not being perfect people? What does that say about you?

15

Fog

The lapis lazuli skies over California's wine country are the jewel setting for brilliance of the midsummer sun. Unimpeded by clouds or moisture, the heat bears down on the grapevines like a relentless, pressing iron, shriveling the leaves and baking the earth. This is the perfect growing condition for developing grapes. Under the shimmering heat of 100-degree weather, they plump, ripen, and glisten with climbing sugar counts. By late afternoon, atmospheric physics takes over and, like all hot air, it rises. This high-pressure system, as it ascends, creates a vacuum for a cooler element to drift into town.

Meanwhile, off the coast, the California Current runs from north to south, carrying frigid temperatures from Alaska to Mexico. This is the opposite of the eastern seaboard where the Gulf Stream runs up from the Caribbean to Maine, bringing warm, tropical waters northward. The cool water off California chills the air above its surface. This air is cold, damp, and heavy. It is also nutrient-rich due to upwellings from winds pulling the nitrogen, phosphorus, and other minerals from deep below the surface. This cool air is a low-pressure system.

While the Napa Valley hot air rises, the dense, cooler air off the Pacific swooshes in to fill the void. We see it as fog. The bane of picnics, tourists, and carefully coiffed hairdos, the fog embraces the city of San Francisco and blots out the Golden Gate Bridge. Joggers and dogs magically evaporate as they pound the sand along the shorelines. Fog curls around cable cars dissolving in the distance and muffles the sound of hawkers on Pier 39.

On hillsides, fog oozes along the landscape, trickling down through the evergreen-forested hills like tentacles, finding pockets and dips in terrain. People stop by the roadside at the foot of these hills and take pictures. Other times, fog is the clueless, cloying guest who has overstayed its welcome. Dense, dripping, and defiantly sticking around for weeks, it dashes all hope of ever feeling the welcome warmth of sun on your face.

But fog isn't just a nuisance—it's a necessity for the giant coastal redwoods. California's famous redwoods (*Sequoia sempervirens*) are distributed along its northern coastal region and up into Oregon. These are the tallest trees in the world, reaching heights of 350 feet. All that height requires a lot of water, and California is famous for not raining all summer. None. At. All.

I found this hard to believe when I moved here from the Midwest. In most parts of the United States, you can never plan an event outside without a plan B for rain. There is no way to know months in advance if your celebration or game is going to be rained out. But not so in California. I was astonished when a friend announced that her wedding would take place outside in June. "But what if it rains?" I asked. She laughed. "Don't be ridiculous! In summer, it never rains in California." I learned the song is true.

But these giant redwoods need water to grow—1300 pounds of it, or two-thirds of a ton, each day. If it doesn't rain all summer, where do they get the water they need? *Sequoia sempervirens* are able to get 25 to 40 percent of their water from fog. As the nutrient-rich moisture billows in from the sea, it feeds and protects the redwoods two ways. First, it covers the leaves to prevent evaporation. Secondly, it enters the tiny pores (stomata) on the leaves and is drawn down through the branches to the roots. This is the opposite of the normal way moisture flows in trees—transpiration—where moisture is pulled up from the roots and evaporated through the leaves. In the coastal redwood, water is able to flow both directions.

And the fog doesn't just benefit the redwoods—it's crucial to the whole forest ecosystem. Some of the moisture from fog drips off these giant trees to water the trees and saplings underneath. This may seem like a small amount—just a few drips—but collectively, it gets down to 35 centimeters, over a foot, in depth. So newts, salamanders, frogs, slugs, snails, insects, and all the critters that feed on them benefit as well. This fog that we see as death to our dreams of outdoor dining is life to forest dwellers.

Summer in San Francisco means fog. One often hears it said, "The coldest winter I ever experienced was a summer in San Francisco!"—and we locals laugh, but it's true. While most of the nation warms up under the summer sun, the San Francisco Bay Area can get surprisingly chilly due to the fog that rolls in most afternoons.

> This fog that we see as death to our dreams of outdoor dining is life to forest dwellers.

You can always tell a tourist in San Francisco. They are shivering on the sidewalks in their brightly colored summer dresses or Hawaiian shirts, shorts, and sandals. They are looking around in bewilderment, trying to hold their hair in place as the wind slaps it into their eyes, fringed with moisture-beaded eyelashes. They frown at the residents bustling by in puffy down parkas. It doesn't seem to compute.

It doesn't make sense. This is summer in California! Where is the sun? This is cold! This isn't at all what they expected from their vacation. They feel ripped off and disappointed.

Once you've spun around the sun a few times, you become acutely aware that things often don't go as planned. And like most people, I have definite ideas about how the script for my life should go. It starts with being raised by perfect, God-fearing parents, who lavished me with security and love and were never too busy to attend to my fears or needs. Then I leave college with a handsome, God-fearing man on my arm who was also raised by perfect parents (so neither of us has any baggage or lifelong issues to deal with). Our careers are fulfilling, and the sky's the limit for our advancement. I easily get pregnant when I want to, and we have three lovely children who come out of the womb saying, "Thy will be done." We live in a darling home and never worry about payments and rising interest rates. There is never devastating news, no surprises, no financial setbacks or illnesses that derail dreams. Sounds pretty fine, right? But as we all discover, we are not in control. And for some of us, the surprises of life, the disorienting devastations that we didn't plan for or expect, can take months or years of adjustment.

I guess I'm a slow learner (or stupidly stubborn) because it took me seven years to lay down my will and accept God's plan for my life.

It started when I married Tom. He was more than a decade older than I was and already had three grown kids. He also had a vasectomy when he was younger. When we married, I knew that we would need some science to get pregnant. But I was confident, even arrogant, that we could surmount any obstacle to my dreams. One embarrassing scene that is imprinted indelibly on my memory is an afternoon in

San Francisco. We were standing by the elevators outside the UCSF medical building. The fog was roaring in and whipping our coats about our knees. We were going up to our doctor's office to start IVF procedures. "What if it doesn't work?" asked Tom.

I laughed and tossed back my hair. "Are you kidding? With my All-American swimmer genes and your PhD in physics genes? We can *sell* the embryos we don't use!" And I punched the up button with the same force and vigor that I approached most challenges in life. Such was my ignorant, calloused, and entitled attitude before I entered the school of suffering.

It took dashed adoption opportunities, three operations for him, hundreds of needles for me, and many IVF cycles over seven years before I finally held our son. My view of God was forever altered when no amount of good behavior or prayer and fasting could get me what I wanted the way I wanted it. Everything I had assumed about who God is and the way He works in our lives was upended. And it wasn't pretty.

While some believers claim they were never mad at God when their husband left them or their child was murdered or their dreams were devastated, I had the opposite reaction. I was furious. He who ordered the planetary forces in their courses and could split the Red Sea could surely do this small thing for me. So why didn't He? I was consumed with self-pity and fury, and felt utterly abandoned by God. The news was full of high school girls getting pregnant and tossing their babies in Dumpsters. Or crack mothers delivering crack-addicted babies. Nothing added up. It was crazy-making and disorienting. If I were running the world, things would not be this way. I had better, kinder, more sensible plans.

My view of God was forever altered when no amount
of good behavior or prayer and fasting could get me
what I wanted the way I wanted it.

Dr. James Dobson describes the temptation to give in to this "bitter barrier." He points out how some people, when faced with a tremendous setback or tough situation, will give up and sit down. They can't—or won't—get over the betrayal and bitterness they feel at how things have turned out. They slump down next to that barrier wall, stick their thumb in their mouth, and sulk, cry, rage, and become helpless with despair.

I know this feeling well. I sat there for seven years pouting. But it didn't help me. The one thing my stubbornness did for me that was positive: I decided to stop being a victim, to stop being stuck. I didn't want to end up forever huddled against my bitter barrier. I wanted to move forward. That meant moving forward in forgiveness toward God, myself, my husband, the dog, and whatever and whomever I raged at. That meant leaning into the God I was furious at and dropping my whys and asking, "What's next?"

Why? keeps us looking at God's hand. It keeps us going in circles, lost in a fog of despair. *What's next?* directs our gaze upward to God's face. It opens the door to the future and gets us moving forward.

Michele Cushatt is a professional speaker with a heart for God. In her books and her blog, *Making Peace with an Imperfect Life*, she chronicles her struggles with divorce, remarriage, foster children, and two bouts of tongue cancer. I heard her interviewed recently, during which she talked about her thoughts regarding the disorienting fog of tough times, situations that don't make sense, and our relationship with God. Michele said she came to the point where she said to God, "I don't always understand You, but I *need* You more than I need to understand You."

> *Why?* keeps us looking at God's hand.
> *What's next?* directs our gaze upward to God's face.

It encourages me to realize God's "superstars" from the Bible also went through tough times and the fog of disillusionment. King David was told he was going to be king, and then spent many years running from a jealous King Saul, who was trying to kill him. It didn't make sense, and David wet his pillow through with his tears. The apostle Paul, that brilliant defender of the faith, writer of 13 books in the Bible, and steadfast missionary, was beaten, shipwrecked, and imprisoned, but he never wavered in his faith that God is loving and that his own adversities were "momentary light afflictions" compared to the joy that is found in a surrendered life in Christ.

When someone talks about suffering and surviving, I always check their credentials. Was their "suffering" a too-busy schedule? Or a child who died or a spouse who ran off? It makes a difference. If they've traveled through that dark and scary place and have wisdom to share, I sit up and take notes. Like when Paul says in 2 Corinthians 4:7-12:

> But we have this treasure in jars of clay to show that this all-surpassing power is from God and not from us. We are hard pressed on every side, but not crushed; perplexed, but not in despair; persecuted, but not abandoned; struck down, but not destroyed. We always carry around in our body the death of Jesus, so that the life of Jesus may also be revealed in our body. For we who are alive are always being given over to death for Jesus' sake, so that his life may also be revealed in our mortal body. So then, death is at work in us, but life is at work in you.

And there is the nugget: *but life is at work in you.* What we fail to see while we are grasping around through the fog of pain and suffering is that God can and will (if we are willing) work through us and with us. He is growing our faith and blessing others through us as we put to death our plans and surrender to His ways. This process, shared with and witnessed by others, can drip down and saturate their faith. Like Michele Cushatt, like the apostle Paul, like you.

It helps others grow, and our faith grows as we soak up His grace and transpire it to others. And that gives our lives hope, growth, direction, and meaning. No matter what winds assail us. No matter how dark the day. So we too can become giants in the faith.

Exploring Further

1. Whose faith do you admire? Why?
2. What have been some "foggy" times in your life—where things didn't make sense and life didn't turn out how you expected?
3. Have you been impacted by another person's suffering? (This could be from a book or in person.) Have you seen it work for good in others' lives?
4. What parts of Romans 5:1-5 below give you hope? What parts do you struggle with?

> Therefore, since we have been justified through faith, we have peace with God through our Lord Jesus Christ, through whom we have gained access by faith into this grace in which we now stand. And we boast in the hope of the glory of God. Not only so, but we also glory in our sufferings, because we know that suffering produces perseverance; perseverance, character; and character, hope. And hope does not put us to shame, because God's love has been poured out into our hearts through the Holy Spirit, who has been given to us.

16

Starfish

The name is beguiling and hints at magic. Starfish. As if they had spent their allotted time in the heavens, then retired and fizzled down in a sparkling plunge into the sea to reside in the quiet depths with the fishes. Why would they want to trade neighborhoods? Is the ocean a more inviting place than space? Occasionally, starfish wash up on shore so we can look at their helpless estate. Their rosy and golden hues make them look like water-colored accents on our sandy shores. On closer inspection, their arms are limp and soggy underneath. A few tubelike feet on their underside may wave at us in defenseless resignation. And usually we are moved to throw them back into the sea. It seems the right thing to do. They are the darlings of beachcombing parents with children because we know we can touch, pick up, and examine them without fear. Starfish are the lumpy but quaint accessories that charm our coastlines. But starfish are neither stars nor fish. In fact, if you want to be scientifically correct, you call them *sea stars*.

Sea stars belong to a large group of animals called echinoderms. Other echinoderms are sea urchins, sand dollars, and sea cucumbers. These animals have no bones, so they are invertebrates, and their outer (top) covering is tough and sometimes spiny or knobby. They come in a myriad of colors and arm assortments. Usually, you will see the typical five-armed sea star, but some have seven, nine, or ten or more. About 1500 species of sea stars are found around the world oceans, from the tropics to the icy polar regions. They are found flung up on the sand, in tide pools, and as deep as 20,000 feet below the surface. Once, when I was visiting my great uncle on Shaw Island in the San Juan Islands near Seattle, he introduced me to the sunflower sea star.

I've never been quick to wake up. Especially before I realized my thyroid was slow, mornings felt like my blood was clogged molasses not yet pumping, and my brain was half steeped in ether. My brilliant but slightly crazy great uncle had graduated magna cum laude in engineering from Princeton University, designed the hydrofoil water jet propulsion system for Boeing, and was always trying to teach or excite others about cool things in the world. Into his seventies he was an avid tennis player and downhill skier. This morning he bounded up the stairs to my loft with a gigantic sunflower sea star (*pycnopodia helianthoides*) on a cutting board. The orange center blob was about a foot across and, instead of having five arms, it had about 20 crammed around its periphery and drooping over the edges of the board. It indeed looked like a massive, gooey, and alien sunflower and reeked of the briny shore. He waved it under my sleepy eyes and crowed triumphantly, "Look what's for breakfast!"

He was kidding—you never knew with him—but his enthusiasm was infectious. I was enchanted by the diversity and variety of sea stars along his Northwest shores. Some had humorous names like Arctic Cookie Star, Slime Star, and Gunpowder Star. Years later, while snorkeling off the Great Barrier Reef in Australia, I was enchanted by the bright blue sea star *Linckia laevigata* and the one that looks like it has chocolate chips on its back, the horned sea star *Protoreaster nodosus*.

Here on the California coast, I mainly spy ochre sea stars in orange and purple, plus the occasional bright red or orange bat star (so named because of its webbed arms like a bat). Although they look helpless and sweet tossed up upon our beaches, the first clue as to the power of sea stars is when you encounter them in a tide pool or underwater clinging to a rock. Try to pry it off. It will be a struggle. Although not as firmly cemented as barnacles, sea stars with their thousands of suctioning tube feet have formidable staying power. But there's something I find uniquely fascinating about these seemingly passive and mythological gifts from the heavens. The sea star, despite its docile looks and charming shape, is a powerful predator.

Have you ever shucked oysters or clams? It takes a specially designed, sharp oyster knife because of how tightly closed they are. And you better have gloved hands. A chain-mail type of glove that protects you from knife slips and stabs is recommended. So although we need a specialty knife and protected hands to open these tough mollusks, a sea star does not.

Slowly roaming along the sand, rocks, or coral beds, the sea star encounters a tightly closed mussel or scallop. Delicately, it feels along the shell for an opening. The thousands of tiny tubular feet beneath its arms dance along the shell's body, searching, questioning, imploring. The bivalve is slammed shut. No matter. The sea star wraps its body around the meek mollusk and, with its arms on either side of the shell, begins to pull. It is in no hurry. Slowly, slowly, it exerts outward, suctioning pressure until the clam or oyster cannot resist the pull. The shell cracks open, just a tiny slit. But that is enough. Our sea star then extends his stomach outside of his body and into the clam through the tiny opening. Its digestive enzymes soften and destroy the meat inside, and the sea star slurps up its tasty meal. The stomach retreats back out of the shell and into the sea star. Our petite predator has prevailed. Mission accomplished.

The surprising tenacity of the innocuous sea star gives me hope. His example of appearing small, charming, and decorative yet hiding a relentless predatory strength is the ultimate switcheroo. You don't expect it. He's like the little old lady who faithfully shows up at church in her matching sweater set and blue-tinged hair. She appears sweet, harmless, and inoffensive. Nothing to take much notice of; in fact, she's kind of cute. But in her home, when she's alone, she rises up in the full armor of God, like a ninja warrior in prayer. She won't give up, she won't shut up, and she doesn't cease putting the pressure on until she sees victory. This is how we crack tough cases: persistent prayer.

The Bible is full of stories of people who engaged in persistent prayer. They applied steady pressure and refused to give up, no matter how tough the case looked. Just like our little sea star.

James 5:16-18 gives us the example of Elijah: "The earnest prayer of a righteous person has great power and produces wonderful results. Elijah was as human as we are, and yet when he prayed earnestly that no rain would fall, none fell for three and a half years! Then, when he prayed again, the sky sent down rain and the earth began to yield its crops" (NLT).

I love that phrase, "Elijah was as human as we are." It's so easy to imagine these people mentioned in the Bible as so much holier, sinless, without envy, pride, or ambition. However, they too were riddled with holes, habits, and humiliations. God isn't looking for perfect prayers but persistent prayers. God moved as a result of Elijah's persistent prayer.

God isn't looking for perfect prayers, but persistent prayers.

We don't have to look back hundreds or thousands of years for examples of persistent prayer producing wonderful results. The Berlin Wall came down as a result of prayer. Ronald Reagan is not responsible for this historic event. Although you can watch the video clips on YouTube where he says, "Mr. Gorbachev, tear down this wall!" and while it all looks historic, epic, and moving, a greater movement happened just behind those walls inside a small church in the East German city of Leipzig beginning seven years earlier, in 1982.

> Tired of the Berlin Wall, the ongoing Cold War and the repressive East German regime, a faithful pastor began organizing Prayers for Peace every Monday evening at St Nicholas church.
>
> On many occasions fewer than a dozen people attended the prayer meetings. The East German government strongly discouraged its citizens from becoming involved in religious activities, but the meetings continued each Monday without fail.[1]

By 1985, the thriving prayer group was growing in earnest. A sign, "Open to All," was put outside, and attendance was exploding. On October 9, 1989, the police were in riot gear warning the pastor and all citizens the price they would pay. The East German police—the Stassi—were notorious for their iron fist. Nothing would be tolerated. But 70,000 praying people filled the streets holding candles. No massacre happened. The East German president, Erich Honecker, resigned. One month later, the Berlin Wall came down. Remember our verse from James? "The earnest prayer of a righteous person has great power and produces wonderful results" (James 5:16).

"All I can do is pray," is what we say after we've called all our friends, consulted with spouses, eaten half of the refrigerator contents, bitten our nails to the quick, and sunk into despair. Prayer shouldn't be a passive folding of the hands, a whimpering murmuring with an unbelieving heart. It can be, when faced with daunting opposition. But prayer can be proactive, wielding the sword of truth—God's Word, the Bible.

I love the movie *War Room*. In it, a little old lady instructs a younger woman how to pray God's Word over her tough situations. The "war room" is her little prayer closet. In it she posts pages of her prayers for her family written out with accompanying Scripture verses. Like the unassuming pastor in Leipzig, we can pray down mighty walls. Figuratively and literally.

When people say "What difference will it make?" it's insulting to the faithful prayer warriors who have modeled steadfast prayer for us throughout the Bible. It can make all the difference. Can you think or speak? Then you are capable of wielding great power.

When Jesus asked Peter, "Who do you say I am?" and Peter said, "You are the Christ, the Messiah," Jesus announced that upon this confession, this bedrock of truth, Jesus would build His church. And then Jesus adds, "And the gates of Hades will not overcome it" (Matthew 16:15-19). Most of us picture ourselves trying to keep hell away from engulfing our lives, our kids, our cities. But here is a picture of the church invading hell's territory and smashing down its gates. We are to advance against these tough situations. We are to move forward in persistent prayer, reach in, and dissolve that evil.

You are not a little, bitty, helpless person who has no friends in higher places. If you are a follower of Jesus Christ, you have God's power on your side. Doesn't matter if you're a little ol' lady, a beleaguered businessman, a maxed-out mother, or a student. Remember our cute, little, squishy starfish? Like a determined predator, surround that tough obstacle and apply the persistent pressure of prayer.

> If you are a follower of Jesus Christ,
> you have God's power on your side.

Prayer is powerful. Jesus depended on it. The disciples relied on it. We can use it to tear down walls, soften hearts, or crack open tough cases. Persistent prayer may sound innocuous and squishy, but it's like a sea star. In tough cases, it's lethal.

Exploring Further

1. Have you ever touched or held a starfish? Where was it? Did anything about it surprise you?
2. What situations do you pray about that seem impossible?
3. When have you witnessed the power of prayer to bring down a figurative wall?
4. Read Job 42:2 and Matthew 19:23-26. How can you apply these passages to your situation?

17

Monarch

We carefully closed the set of double doors behind us in a whoosh to make sure the butterflies didn't escape. At first, the humidity stunned me. It was winter, but I was standing in a lush, Amazonian jungle with a parka on. Sweating. But the sharp intake of breath from my son made me look down. A butterfly was landing on his outstretched finger. He barely breathed. The insect leisurely opened and closed its tissue paper wings. Closed, it looked like a brown, dead leaf. Open, it was a startling riot of orange and maroon with black spots. Once, twice, and then he fluttered off. My son turned to me wide-eyed. "Mommy! There's one on your shoulder!"

Mine was a dainty, lavender-blue Spring Azure, with a tidy white edge along its delicate wings. I slowly moved my head to look closer. It coyly showed off its Wedgewood blue finery, and then coasted off. All around us was the confetti of colorful, fragile insects. Hues from a watercolor palette took flight, danced around our heads, and played hide-and-seek with the foliage in our enclosure. It was utterly charming and mesmerizing. We were in the Natural History Museum's butterfly exhibit in New York City.

Butterfly exhibits have become increasingly popular for museums and arboretum centers. The first one, established in 1976, was the London Butterfly House in Middlesex, England. It was a huge success, with hundreds of exotic species, but sadly was demolished by the Duke of Northumberland to build a hotel complex. However, there are other amazing butterfly houses around the world. In England, there's now the Stratford Butterfly Farm in Stratford-upon-Avon. There are also noteworthy exhibits in Austria, Australia, Germany, Malaysia, Singapore, and Canada. Closer to home, there is the huge Butterfly Pavilion in Westminster, Colorado, with 7200 square feet to delight in. Niagara Parks Butterfly Conservatory boasts over 2000 butterflies and 45 species. And the biggest one in the United States is Butterfly World in Coconut Creek, Florida. Started in 1988 by Ronald Boender (who was inspired by the former London Butterfly House), it has 150 species and works with the University of Florida to reintroduce endangered species like the Schaus swallowtail.

You'll find many smaller butterfly exhibits not mentioned in travel sites tucked here and there around the US. I've been in charming butterfly exhibits in San Francisco's Golden Gate Park and Olbrich Botanical Gardens in Madison, Wisconsin. Not only is it mesmerizing to watch a butterfly escape from its cocoon—or chrysalis—but these centers are also full of information about the care and feeding of butterflies and how to entice them to your yard.

As much as I love experiencing these butterfly houses, I think it is more thrilling to catch a glimpse of a butterfly by chance, when you least expect it, outside. My most memorable sighting was up in Australia's rain forest near Cairns. Although I had lived there for three years, I had never managed to see this part of the country. So for my fortieth birthday, my husband flew me back to my beloved sunburnt country to the Great Barrier Reef. On the way, we spent a few days in the rain forest.

Think of the most intense downpour you've ever seen. Now double it. And maybe, double it again. "Cats and dogs," buckets, even bathtubs don't adequately describe the amount and intensity of water that gushes down in a rain forest. It was more like a constant, intense waterfall. One afternoon, during a short break in the rain, I went out for a walk. The humidity was so penetrating, it felt like a swim. But I wanted to have a look around at all the lush jungle greenery.

Out of the corner of my eye, I caught an intense, blue flash. I looked again. The brilliant, cyan blue Ulyssess butterfly was erratically swooping by with his enormous five-inch wingspan. The blue is so intense, it's hard to describe. But the best I can do is compare it to an iridescent swatch of electric blue offset by a dramatic scalloped edging of velvet black. Ulysses was the rarest and biggest butterfly I have ever seen, and the experience was totally thrilling.

While we don't have the tropical Ulysses butterfly here in the US, there are secretive sites where you can have inspiring moments with the dramatic orange and black migrating monarchs. In these mysterious hideaways, you can view them by the thousands, sometimes millions. Here they cluster in the trees, covering them so that the tree leaves appear to be made with butterfly wings.

- Point Pelee National Park, Ontario, Canada
- Monarch Butterfly Grove, Pismo Beach, California
- Monarch Sanctuary Grove, Pacific Grove, California
- Goleta Monarch Butterfly Grove, Goleta, California
- Natural Bridges State Beach, Santa Cruz, California
- Monarch Biosphere Reserve, Michoacán, Mexico
- Piedra Herrada, Los Saucos, Mexico

Our family went to the Natural Bridges State Beach to see them one winter day. We walked down the wooden boardwalk ramp into a dense grove of eucalyptus trees. It was a weekday, and there had been a break in the drizzly, cold weather. The sun was out, and I had heard that this was the perfect sort of day for viewing.

There were a few butterflies flitting about, but I thought, *Where are the thousands I heard about? This is a bit of a disappointment!* Then I noticed the people ahead of me. Their necks were craned back as if they were expecting something to fall from the sky. I looked up. The trees towering above us were covered with thousands upon thousands of orange and black wings. Every so often a breeze would make the branches sway, and hundreds of stained-glass wings would lift off and wink about in the sunshine. It was like being at a wedding or memorial event where they let loose clouds of butterflies, and the sight of them makes your heart soar upward. There was a collective *ooooohhhhing* and *ahhhhhing* from us admirers gazing up at them in adoration.

> Every so often a breeze would make the branches sway, and hundreds of stained-glass wings would lift off and wink about in the sunshine.

When I was a child in the Midwest, there seemed to be monarchs in every garden. Bold orange, black, and white Tiffany lampshade wings would be gliding about in nearly everyone's yard. They were as common as daisies. I wondered why I saw them so many years ago but now hardly ever saw them when I came back in the summer. Where had all the monarchs gone?

The middle of the United States, the "corn belt," like Iowa, Missouri, and Kansas, used to be wild prairies. These prairies were covered with native wildflowers that are the food for monarchs. For years, the farming techniques that plowed up the earth left a little bit of wildness on the corners and fencerows of the planted acres. The machinery couldn't get into those edges. And in those pockets, monarchs could feed, breed, and thrive. But today, systemic pesticides and new technology have allowed farmers to cultivate every square inch of their fields, leaving nothing untouched. Thus, we are losing 6000 acres a day of potential habitat. I was stunned to learn they might be facing extinction. We have lost approximately 90 percent of our monarch population! They are important pollinators, like bees, not just a pretty, nice-to-have adornment to our yards. The Environmental Defense Fund (EDF) puts it this way:

> Over the past two decades, the population of monarch butterflies has plummeted, bringing the butterfly dangerously close to extinction. A key factor in the monarch's demise is the loss of milkweed habitat across the United States, particularly in the Midwest. Milkweed has long found a foothold in both native prairie habitats and in disturbed habitats like roadsides, ditches, cemeteries, and even in the middle of cornfields. But the monarch is losing this foothold due largely to increased use of herbicides in agriculture, and additional threats posed by climate change.[1]

So, while visiting butterfly exhibits or viewing them in their migrating rest stops is delightful, learning how to attract monarchs and provide for them is becoming a matter of survival. Their continued existence depends on us. And this can be a fun opportunity for families to do something positive, educational, and beautiful.

While the EDF works with companies and ranchers to provide habitats, homeowners, schools, and libraries can be an important link for the monarch's survival as well.

This is where the Monarch Waystation movement comes in. Monarchs migrate a shockingly long way for such a fragile creature—from the Great Lakes in Canada to central Mexico—2500 miles. And along the way, they need to fuel up. MonarchWatch.org is a site where you can learn about what it takes to create a certified way-station for these butterflies. Although the site is a bit cluttered, it contains solid information and links where you can find milkweed seeds (their favorite plant) and education about how and why to create a safe resting stop for the monarch butterfly. There is also information for educators to use in their classrooms, as well as home gardening tips.

Without our help, I doubt these amazing creatures will make it. They will just flutter their wings once, twice, and then fall quietly to the ground. There was no audible cry when the last of the billions of passenger pigeons went extinct. There was no announcement when the gorgeous Carolina parakeet breathed its last breath. It will be a quiet tragedy if the monarch butterfly disappears from our land. Those of us who love nature can stand in the gap for these vulnerable creatures that can't speak for themselves.

There are a lot of vulnerable situations asking for our support these days. And sometimes the need is so great that it feels overwhelming. Particularly, the defenseless women and children out on our streets. It's easy to dismiss them and think, "You made your choices." And if I'm honest, I sometimes think these dark, uncharitable, and selfish thoughts. But do they really have a choice?

For most of these women roaming our streets today, their choices are bleak. They have to make choices like, stay with this foster family where I'm being raped, or get out and try to live on the streets? Stay with my drug-addicted parent where I'm getting beat up and threatened by her boyfriend? Or leave for something hopefully better?

Some have been drugged, kidnapped, and threatened with death if they leave. And some have told their families that they are confused about their gender, or gay, and have been kicked out on the streets. The choice was made for them. Once they are on their own and desperate for love and belonging, they often end up in sex trafficking. Children's bodies are bought and sold. This is not a life they would *choose* for themselves.

I am in the middle of reading a really difficult book. I keep wanting to put it down. The details are so sad, sordid, and depressing. I don't want to know all this. I don't want to be acquainted with such grief. Rachel Lloyd's book *Girls Like Us* opens with her talking to a young girl who has come in off of the streets, trying to get out of "the life." After chatting with her a bit, Rachel discovers that this young woman is 11. Eleven years old! This is not technically a young woman. This is a *child*. But increasingly, children (who are younger and younger) are ending up on the streets, starved for love, family, or just a warm place to stay. Then they get entrapped. They have no one who truly cares about them or will rescue them. They get sold and used repeatedly, sometimes through several states. In the land of the free and the brave, slavery is an active and profitable business. These kids are not free, and they need someone brave.

When I consider these kids, I am haunted by this passage in Proverbs:

> Rescue those being led away to death;
>   hold back those staggering toward slaughter.
> If you say, "But we knew nothing about this,"
>   does not he who weighs the heart perceive it?
> Does not he who guards your life know it?
>   Will he not repay everyone according to what they
>   have done?
> (Proverbs 24:11-12).

Thankfully, there are organizations stepping up to raise awareness and stem this tide. There are more than I will mention here. These two are just to get you started.

GEMS—Girls Educational & Mentoring Services was founded in 1998 by Rachel Lloyd, author of *Girls Like Us*. Based in New York State, GEMS was created in response to "an overwhelming need for services for girls and young women at risk for commercial sexual exploitation and domestic trafficking who were being ignored by traditional social service agencies."[2] They also lobbied for passage of the Safe Harbor Act for Sexually Exploited Youth. Meaning, not treating girls under 16 as criminals but as victims. Read Rachel's book for a full understanding of how children and young women become entrapped in this cycle.

A21 is a worldwide ministry founded by Christine Caine.[3] The name represents their mission to abolish in the twenty-first century all forms of slavery. They are involved with rescuing girls, helping to work with prosecutors, prevention, and global awareness. They specialize in aftercare to help victims get a foothold psychologically, socially, and spiritually. They help them to see themselves as a worthy and important part of society. They assist them in getting training for meaningful employment. Without this kind of support, statistics are that 80 percent will be re-trafficked. They have many firsthand video accounts on their website that will chill you to the bone. This could be your daughter or niece. *Rescue, Restore, and Rebuild* are their watchwords.

I find it astounding that after the work of Lincoln, Wilberforce, and Martin Luther King Jr., slavery is thriving and more robust than ever in this country. Right under our noses. It crosses races and gender. Black, white, Filipino, African, girls, boys, men, and women are all equal opportunity victims.

But maybe in your neighborhood, in your church, there aren't these global issues. Maybe there are "smaller" victims who need your protection. Who is the kid at school that everyone bullies and picks on? Who gets chosen last for every game? Who wears the same clothes every day? Maybe your family could be a friend, or leave clothes with a teacher, or pay a child's way to camp. Each of us can make a small difference to show someone cares. We can start within our own circles of influence. And we can provide anything: time, tangible resources, or shelter. When we create waystations of refuge, we create opportunities for healing and growth.

It doesn't take much. Years ago, I had a girlfriend show up at our house with her car packed to the roof with most of her belongings. Instead of divorcing her husband, she needed a break. Although we were accused of aiding and abetting, we took her in and provided a safe haven. We let her work through her issues. She returned to her husband months later, refreshed and refueled.

> When we create waystations of refuge,
> we create opportunities for
> healing and growth.

As we plant our milkweed seeds for the monarchs and create a waystation of refuge for them in their journey, maybe we could think about how to be a refuge for someone else. Let's pray about who needs a break, who needs someone to step in, who needs a waystation that we can provide.

Exploring Further

1. What is your favorite butterfly? Have you ever visited a living exhibit?

2. Have you ever had an encounter with butterflies in the wild? Or seen them emerge from their chrysalis?

3. Be honest with yourself. What is your first reaction when you see women living on the streets? Do you have the same uncharitable thoughts as the author?

4. When have you felt your freedom threatened? Consider one small effort you can make toward helping an organization or individual who experiences that threat daily.

5. How does the passage in Proverbs (on page 165) make you feel? Is there someone in your life who needs a short "waystation" that you could provide?

18

Bluebird

The drive took us 25 white-knuckled minutes to reach the property at the top of the mountain. Our real-estate agent kept turning around to talk with us while she negotiated hairpin turns with heart-stopping drop-offs. After we crossed a stream, gunned vertical climbs that made San Francisco look like a bunny hill, and survived axle-twisting ruts and bumps, I was just thankful to have made it alive, never mind the fantastic scenery. But what distracted my stomach from turning itself inside out upon our arrival was the cheery bluebird that flew straight to our car and perched itself on our side mirror. While my husband sucked in his breath at the view of the Pacific Ocean, my head was turned to watch our cute welcoming agent.

A bluebird! I thought, definitely a wonderful omen for this property. I hadn't seen any bluebirds growing up in Wisconsin (not that I was looking for them) and was utterly charmed by this visitation. He cocked his head, looked around, sang to us a little, and gazed at himself in our mirrors. While the real-estate agent waxed on about the property and its benefits, I stood transfixed by our blue-feathered visitor with his plump red breast. Despite the fact that he left copious amounts of digestive evidence on the car by the time he fluttered off, I was thrilled that the proverbial bluebird of happiness came with the property.

Later, when I remarked about our unique feathered visitor to our neighbor Peter, he said, "Oh, well, of course, the reason we have so many bluebirds up here is because of the bluebird trail we set up." *Bluebird trail?* I had never heard of this.

According to Donald and Lillian Stokes (they have authored many books on birding), the first bluebird trail was created by Thomas E. Musselman when he placed birdhouses along stretches of a road. In the 1920s and 1930s, he could see the native bluebird was getting crowded out of prime nesting areas by the imported European house sparrows and starlings. So in 1934, Musselman started a "bluebird trail." Eventually, he had a trail of more than one thousand boxes in Adams County, Illinois. Around the same time, William Duncan set up bluebird trails in Jefferson County, Kentucky, and also created a great basic bluebird nest box. These two efforts were the beginning of bluebird conservation. Thanks to hundreds of Americans across the country who are putting up bluebird trails and making their backyards a haven for them, bluebirds are slowly growing from sparse populations to more abundant ones.

You can learn more about how to create and maintain a bluebird trail by reading the Stokes's book *The Bluebird Book* or by visiting the Bluebird Society website. However, you don't need a bluebird trail to encourage the bluebird of happiness to come to your backyard— just provide the right environment. In the summer, bluebirds need bluebird houses (these have specific measurements to deter other birds and predators; see the Stokes's book), a lot of insects, and low vegetation so they can find those insects. Therefore, blasting your yard with chemicals to kill all bugs will ensure you have no blue-birds. They hunt for these insects from perches, so make sure you have some bushes, chairs, or other areas where they can perch. Blue-birds also enjoy berry-producing trees, shrubs, and vines. Your local nursery will know what grows best in your area. In the winter, these berry-producing plants are vital to their survival as they provide shel-ter as well.

Not only do bluebirds enjoy insects and berries, but they also love mealy worms. When I was in Wisconsin, my mother and I were visiting a wonderful birding store. A young woman walked in and ordered lots of mealy worms. "What do you feed with those?" I asked her. "Bluebirds," she sighed. "They practically go through a box a day, but how can you say no to *bluebirds?*"

Why do we work so hard to create conditions for the bluebird to grace our yards? What is it about this charming little bird that warms our heart, thrills us when we see it, and imparts this charming affili-ation with happiness?

Bluebirds have long been associated with good luck and happi-ness. Henry David Thoreau said, "The bluebird carries the sky on his back." Many greeting cards start out with, "May the bluebird of happiness..." In the movie *The Wizard of Oz*, Dorothy sings about a better place she'd like to escape to—over the rainbow where dreams come true—a place where bluebirds fly.

> Bluebirds have long been associated with good luck and happiness.

We've all felt like that at times. When the economy is stumbling, my husband doesn't know if he can keep up with the demands at work, and my hopes and dreams never seem to materialize, I too would like to fly over the rainbow to a happier, saner place. Whether it's over the rainbow or over the next fence, we are convinced it's better anywhere but here. My friends' lives all look simpler and happier to me; their homes are tidier, and their bodies are trimmer. I frequently have to remind myself not to swallow the lie that they are happier than I am. That may or may not be true, but it's probably not due to what they possess compared to what I lack.

Happiness is big business in America. Indeed, we think it is our God-given right. The Declaration of Independence pronounces that our mission statement as a country is "…Life, liberty and the pursuit of happiness." Popular speaker Tony Campolo states that while most Japanese parents would say they want their children to be successful, most Americans, when asked what they want for their children, will sigh and say, "I just want them to be *happy*."

Most of us would like to be happy all the time, and we will go to great lengths to ensure that the bluebird of happiness sits on our shoulder. We change our spouses or jobs or homes. We get our thighs sucked, tummies tucked, and faces lifted. We "shop till we drop," overindulge at the table, and fill our glasses too many times. How do I know this? Because I am guilty of some of these (and others I frequently consider).

Our media convey the message that if we marry the right person, if we get the right job, if our children would do the right thing, if we could move to a bigger home, lose that weight, we would *find* happiness. It's ironic to me we're all chasing this land of never-never, this Atlantis called Happiness. I find it ironic because we are living in the world's most prosperous nation, yet the whole culture is set up that, in order to maintain the economy, people need to keep buying things. We are fed the lie that we don't possess enough talent, we aren't attractive enough, and we don't have enough stuff. I know this because I used to work in advertising, and every ad campaign we thought of started out with creating the perception of a need (that only our product could fill). Like gerbils on the exercise wheel, we can never reach this destination or fill this Grand Canyon of need.

I saved a greeting card I bought years ago. I never gave it to anyone because I felt the message was for me. Me, who constantly compared what I had to what others had and always found myself lacking. It was a quotation attributed to Abraham Lincoln: "Most people are as happy as they make up their minds to be."

I like this quotation because it points out that the state of happiness isn't something we run after, hoping it descends on us. It's a state of mind we *choose*. We can choose to be content with what we have and who we are.

> Happiness isn't something we run after;
> it's a state of mind we *choose*.

Research backs up this idea. According to *The Journal of Happiness Studies*, edited by sociology professor Ruut Veenhoven of Erasmus University, Rotterdam, the single most important factor in someone's state of happiness is close ties to friends and family. Wealth did not matter as much as this factor. Climate or country did not matter as much either.

Establishing close ties with friends and family doesn't just happen. It takes work. It's a choice. Ask anyone on the third day of Thanksgiving vacation. It's amazing how easily family members can hit your hot buttons and annoy you with unerring accuracy. My mother made a humorous needlepoint pillow that was in her guest room asking, "You *are* leaving by Sunday, aren't you?"

Marriage seminars point out that love is, most of the time, not a feeling but a choice. I don't always feel ooey-gooey toward my husband. Sometimes, in the middle of a disagreement, we don't even like each other much, but we are committed to loving each other. People often ask us, "How did you find each other? You have such a good marriage!" They have the erroneous belief that there is a lot of love in our marriage because we just happened to have found the right person. I don't think it's because we found the right person; it's because we are willing to make the right *choices*. Choices to drop our pride and say, "I'm sorry; I was wrong. You were right." Choices to put the other person first and do what *they* want to do this Saturday. Choices to not compare our spouse unfavorably with another's spouse.

Wise King Solomon also talked about happiness, or contentment, as being the product of right choices. In the book of Ecclesiastes he says, "To enjoy your work and accept your lot in life—this is indeed a gift from God. God keeps such people so busy enjoying life that they take no time to brood over the past" (Ecclesiastes 5:19-20 NLT). This concept is stated again in 1 Timothy 6:6-8, "But godliness with contentment is great gain. For we brought nothing into the world, and we can take nothing out of it. But if we have food and clothing, we will be content with that." This is the opposite message we are getting from the world around us, which is, *What we don't have will make us happy—go for it—just do it.* These scriptures are telling us that happiness is choosing to enjoy what we have and being thankful for it.

Author Anne Lamott talks about a friend of hers named Paul. He's in his eighties and has the right outlook on life. He says, "I try to enjoy life the way it is because that's the way it's going to be anyway." How different this approach is from my usual response of anger and power struggles to try to change things to my liking.

I easily fall into the trap of thinking, *It's not fair. I don't have things when other less responsible women do.* My girlfriend struggles with thinking, *It's not fair. Others have a home when we are stuck in a tiny apartment. We would use it for serving others!* Since we both struggle with this comparison problem, I posted the following saying in my bathroom where I'd see it often. It's the recipe for contentment from a missionary who knew hard times. These words keep me from lapsing into that mistaken state of entitlement that thinks, *I should have this. It's my right. Everyone else does*, and points my chooser in the right direction.

> *Never allow yourself to complain about anything—not even the weather.*
>
> *Never picture yourself in any other circumstances or anywhere else.*
>
> *Never compare your lot with another's.*
>
> *Never allow yourself to wish this or that had been otherwise.*
>
> *Never dwell on tomorrow—remember that tomorrow is God's, not ours.*
>
> E.B. PUSEY

I'll admit that sometimes I think these words are impossible to follow and a little extreme. But I notice on days when I'm counting my blessings, enjoying the gifts of friendship, good health, and loving others, *I'm happy*. It's not a result of anything I purchased or achieved or a place I traveled to. It's the result of right choices.

Soon, I'm going to my local wild bird store to buy some bluebird boxes. This, combined with the fruit-bearing shrubs I intend to plant, will create the conditions to encourage bluebirds to visit my home. When visitors sigh and say, "Oh, how lucky you are! You have the bluebird of happiness visiting your home!" I'll say, "Luck has nothing to do with it. I chose to have them, and so can you."

Exploring Further

1. What is your immediate go-to for eliminating feelings of anxiety? Is it something you eat? Or something you do, like shopping? When did this habit start?
2. Who in your life seems to have the happiness you would like?
3. What fallacies do you believe would make you happy? What situation?
4. Do you know anyone who has chosen to be happy despite circumstances?

19

Mountain Lion

Sam put his feet up on the weathered wooden bench and grunted. "A coyote got another calf today," he said, adjusting his cap and leaning back in the chair. I frowned. "How do you know it was a coyote?" I asked. "You've got both coyotes and mountain lions around here killing things. How do you know which one did it?"

Sam is a ranch manager for a friend of mine. He oversees hundreds of acres, cattle, horses, sheep, and all the farming vehicles and staff. He's a busy guy. Today my husband and I were sitting outside under the oak trees with Sam, talking about the goings-on around the place. A lot of rural California has mountain lions (or, as they are commonly called, cougars, pumas, and panthers), as well as coyotes spread about the hills. And I was curious how he could tell which animal had done the deed. He smiled at my question and leaned forward.

"I've seen both kinds of kill sites here. Now, when a coyote kills an animal, it's a mess. The animal is tugged at and ripped apart. There are leg bones over here, tail pulled off over there, it looks like a tug of war or a pillow fight or something." He waved his hands in the air demonstrating a chaotic killing site. "And they start eating it at

any old place, usually the backend, whatever. But it's totally different with a mountain lion. They're very precise. They approach it like
a surgeon."

Sam went on to describe the precise way mountain lions deal with
their victims. First they take down their prey with a bite to the neck
and jugular area. They're strong enough to snap the spine or wind-
pipe. Then once the animal is down, they neatly chew off the hair,
like in an operating room where they shave the spot that's going to
be opened. Then they carefully focus on the chest area—the internal organs first. They neatly open it up, laying the skin apart like a
tidy envelope. They chew through the ribs to get at the most nutri-
tious parts—heart, lungs, and liver. Finally, they drag it to a spot
where they can conceal it and come back to it later for more. Sam
leaned back. "Coyotes just leave their kill out in the open. They're
slobs. But not a mountain lion." He shook his head. "They're cun-
ning and stealthy."

A shiver went through me as I remembered reading about a high
school boy in Colorado years ago. He went out for a solitary run near
his school around 1:00 in the afternoon and disappeared. They found
him a day later. He wasn't all mauled; in fact, he looked like he was
sleeping. But he had been dragged under some brush and his insides
neatly eaten. He had been killed by a mountain lion.

I think about these facts whenever I want to go meandering in the
hills for a hike. I never go alone. Although people will tell me attacks
usually happen at night, and I needn't worry, I remember that boy,
running around his high school at one in the afternoon. And then I
have the data point of my friend Stephanie. She saw a mountain lion
in her driveway at three in the afternoon.

Oftentimes, people mistake a bobcat sighting for a mountain lion. A bobcat is a little bigger than a chunky house cat, but like his name says, he does not have much of a tail. It is "bobbed," a little, short thing. You'll know a mountain lion because he has a long tail, two to three feet long. So from nose tip to tail, a male can be about six to eight feet long. And they can weigh from 120 to 220 pounds. Also, a bobcat's coat is multicolored, orangish with black spots, somewhat like a tabby cat. A mountain lion is a solid tawny color. But when you only get a brief glimpse of an animal, the easiest thing to look for is a tail.

Bobcats feed on rodents, such as rabbits or gophers, and while a mountain lion will eat them too, he prefers bigger game, like deer. Once he takes down a deer, the mountain lion will feast for a while and then cover it up with pine needles or whatever is around so he can come back to it later and feed. If you are out hiking and encounter a half-eaten animal that's partially covered up, I wouldn't stick around. That's his cache, or pantry, and he won't take kindly to you messing with it.

According to the mountainlion.org website, they have formidable skills.

Mountain lions can:

- Bound up to 40 feet running
- Leap 15 feet up a tree
- Climb over a 12 foot fence
- Travel many miles at 10 mph
- Reach speeds of 50 mph in a sprint[1]

So every time I hike with someone who hasn't been to my friend's ranch before, I warn them about what to do if we are approached by a mountain lion.

- Stand tall, wave your arms over your head, open your jacket. Try to appear as big as possible. Do not bend over. *Do not run!* This will mark you as prey, and the chase is on.
- Speak in a commanding, loud, low voice. (Shrill, high sounds are what wounded rabbits and foxes make, so speak low.)
- Act defiant and aggressive. Throw stones, stare him down.
- Back away very slowly.

Mountain lions are ambush hunters; they lie in wait and pounce on their victims unaware. I used to think I had to look up into trees or high places when I hiked, and probably looked quite ridiculous constantly cranking my neck back looking into every tree. But they don't like to be airborne when they attack. They want both back feet on the ground for maneuverability and stability. So instead of constantly scanning my environment for something to pounce on me, I never hike alone, and I always keep aware of my surroundings.

This is good advice for most of life. Stick with others and stay aware. I do it when I'm in a crowded place, such as movie theaters or stadiums. I always check where the exits are and plan my escape in case of earthquake, fire, or crazed gunman. Sticking with others and staying aware is a good strategy spiritually as well. Because whether or not we see it or notice it, there is an enemy just waiting for you to trip up so he can pounce on you.

The apostle Peter warns us about this, "Be alert and of sober mind. Your enemy the devil prowls around like a roaring lion looking for someone to devour. Resist him, standing firm in the faith, because you know that the family of believers throughout the world is undergoing the same kind of sufferings" (1 Peter 5:8-9).

It's interesting that Peter doesn't mention governments or people who oppose him. He sees the real source to be feared—the enemy of our souls. Most people try to pinpoint the enemy as a person or group of people. Peter acknowledges the true enemy. This isn't the first time the Bible talks about this. Paul writes in the book of Ephesians, "For our struggle is not against flesh and blood, but against the rulers, against the authorities, against the powers of this dark world and against the spiritual forces of evil in the heavenly realms" (Ephesians 6:12).

Contrary to popular, positive thinking, we are not getting better as a species. Just look at the daily news. We have terrorist attacks and high school shootings and all sorts of evil in our society. The writers of popular movie scripts may scoff at the idea of a singular, sinister entity, but that's just where the enemy wants us.

> Be alert and of sober mind. Your enemy the
> devil prowls around like a roaring lion looking
> for someone to devour (1 Peter 5:8).

C.S. Lewis writes in his book *The Screwtape Letters*, as a senior devil instructing his junior associate devil in how to keep humans attitudes about evil in check:

> I do not think you will have much difficulty in keeping the patient in the dark. The fact that "devils" are predominantly *comic* figures in the modern imagination will help you. If any faint suspicion of your existence begins to arise in his mind, suggest to him a picture of something in red tights, and persuade him that since he cannot believe in that (it is an old textbook method of confusing them) he therefore cannot believe in you.[2]

Even though it is not wearing red tights, there is evil in your local prison, the psychopath down the street, and in your own heart. Believe it.

In response to this, you'll find Christians all over the map. Some see a demon behind every cough and sniffle and seek to cast it out. Some think there might be some sort of spiritual harassment in the world, but maybe in the Middle East or China. And some laugh at the idea of any real, dark entity working against us.

But the Bible makes it clear: There *is* an enemy, and he *is* active in our lives. But we don't need to live in fear. We can do the same thing Jesus did when He encountered temptation and demonic threats.

Immediately after His baptism, Jesus was led out into the wilderness for 40 days. While out there lonely and hungry, He was tempted by Satan. Mary DeMuth, author of *Beautiful Battle: A Woman's Guide to Spiritual Warfare*, points out that Satan's tactics aren't all that original. He tempted Jesus with the same three things that he tempted Eve with and the same things he tempts us with: pleasure, stuff, and achievement. The following is how Luke 4:1-13 (NLT) plays out as Satan tempts Jesus. Jesus shows us how to combat those dark feelings, outright appeals to our ego, and desire for comfort—with God's Word.

Pleasure. When Jesus was hungry, Satan taunted Him, "If you are the Son of God, tell this stone to become a loaf of bread." How did Jesus respond? The same way we can, with the truth of God's Word. Jesus said, "The Scriptures say, 'People do not live by bread alone.'"

Stuff. "The devil took him up and revealed to him all the kingdoms of the world in a moment of time. 'I will give you the glory of these kingdoms and authority over them,' the devil said, 'because they are mine to give to anyone I please. I will give it all to you if you will worship me.'" Again, Jesus refuted him simply with Scripture. "You must worship the LORD your God and serve only him."

Achievement. "Then the devil took him to Jerusalem, to the highest point of the Temple, and said, 'If you are the Son of God, jump off! For the Scriptures say, "He will order his angels to protect and guard you. And they will hold you up with their hands so you won't even hurt your foot on a stone.'"" Jesus didn't do any Marvel movie tricks, He simply responded, "The Scriptures also say, 'You must not test the Lord your God.'"

> We don't need to live in fear. We can do the same thing Jesus did when He encountered temptation and demonic threats.

While most of us aren't going to encounter Satan face-to-face with him offering us the kingdoms of this world, that doesn't mean we aren't encountering demonic activity unawares or in our families.

My friend Sarah's daughter was woken up repeatedly by horrible nightmares one week. After making sure it wasn't based on anything her daughter had seen or been watching online, she thought it was probably the enemy's response to the new prayer ministry at church she had joined. No matter, she knew her tools. Sarah put together a list of prayers that were based on Scripture to combat the evil that was assailing her daughter. It was simply a list of Bible verses that state our authority over the enemy. She gave it to her daughter to pray out loud to combat her fears. It looked something like this:

Thank You, Jesus, that You have "destroyed the works of the devil." Thank You that "You have the keys of death and of Hades." I don't have to be afraid because "Greater is He who is in me than he that is in the world." I am sitting here in victory because at the name of Jesus "every knee shall bow and tongue confess that You are Lord."[3]

What is she doing? The same thing Jesus did when confronted by Satan in the wilderness. Swinging the one offensive weapon in her spiritual armor: God's Word. The enemy cowers and leaves when we use God's Word.

The Word of God is powerful, and we are told to use it as part of our armor. To be on the offensive with it. The apostle Paul writes in the book of Ephesians,

> Finally, be strong in the Lord and in his mighty power. Put on the full armor of God, so that you can take your stand against the devil's schemes. For our struggle is not against flesh and blood, but against the rulers, against the authorities, against the powers of this dark world and against the spiritual forces of evil in the heavenly realms. Therefore put on the full armor of God, so that when the day of evil comes, you may be able to stand your ground, and after you have done everything, to stand. Stand firm then, with the belt of truth buckled around your waist, with the breastplate of righteousness in place, and with your feet fitted with the readiness that comes from the gospel of peace. In addition to all this, take up the shield of faith, with which you can extinguish all the flaming arrows of the evil one. Take the helmet of salvation and the sword of the Spirit, which is the word of God.
>
> And pray in the Spirit on all occasions with all kinds of prayers and requests. With this in mind, be alert and always keep on praying for all the Lord's people (Ephesians 6:10-18).

Notice how all the other parts of the armor are defensive? The belt of truth is where we start, knowing the truth of our position in Christ. The breastplate protects our heart, our beliefs about how much we are loved. The shield of faith to deflect the arrows of, "God doesn't really love you," and, "Who are you to call yourself aligned with Him?" And then the helmet protects our mind, our thinking. Until the last one, the "sword of the Spirit." This is our one offensive weapon.

We don't have to fear this enemy who prowls around, seeking to devour us. Jesus through His death on the cross has already defeated him, as we've seen in these examples. But we must stand our ground. Just as if you are facing a mountain lion, do not cower. Do not run away screaming. Speak sternly to it and use the sword of the Spirit— Bible verses. Proclaim the victory that is yours. It's not about your courage or ability. It's about the finished work of the shed blood of Jesus Christ. That's how you tame a lion.

Exploring Further

1. Have you ever had a time when you felt you were under spiritual attack?
2. What did you do about it?
3. Does talking about spiritual warfare make you nervous or afraid? Why? What about this chapter encourages you and helps you feel braver?
4. What verses here do you think would be a good idea to write down or memorize?

20

Zipline

The brochure said, *"Ziptrek is home to the longest zipline in Canada & the USA... The Sasquatch is the longest at 7,000 ft long, drops ~1,640 ft over the course of the run, and is 600 ft above the ground at points. It's a true monster! (and fast!)."* Accompanying photographs showed smiling women giving the thumbs-up as they flew along above the treetops. Some pictures showed couples zipping along side by side on parallel lines. It also depicted people heavier than me, so I figured I wouldn't be the one to break the system if it were ever to go down. It was all good.

To me, this was a recipe for fun. To my husband and 12-year-old son, it was a recipe for insanity and probable bodily injury. Where there is excitement, something new, gorgeous scenery, and a once-in-a-lifetime opportunity, I say, "All systems GO!" We may never pass this way again. Grab the moment. Seize the day.

I wasn't a tomboy growing up. Nor was I raised with a band of brothers. But I was raised surrounded by photographs of my grandmother exploring the world. These made an indelible impression on my midwestern mind. There was another world out there, and if my *grandmother* could explore it, then surely I too could have adventures someday.

When my grandfather died unexpectedly and too early, my grandmother took to traveling the world with her best friend, Betty. We saw slides of them in the 60s and 70s, exploring the ancient Cambodian temples of Angkor Wat, covered with primeval vines and before most tourism really got going. In another photo, she was dancing with Balinese dancers in Bali. Trips to temples in India, eating her way through Europe, and learning Ikebana flower arranging in Japan were all on those slides. Anything exotic was her narcotic. And in all these pictures she is smiling broadly, clearly having the time of her life. Her eclectic, artistic, and adventurous life was an inspiration for me.

So when presented with opportunities like roller coasters, rafting, and anything that promises rip-roaring fun, I'm all for it. And the company, Ziptrek, promised me that with their selection of zipline options, I would have a unique experience. We headed to Canada to explore British Columbia and much of its bounty. Vancouver, Victoria, and Whistler were on the agenda. Most people travel to Whistler for the fantastic skiing, but we were going in the summer. So gondola rides to the peaks, ferryboat rides to Vancouver Island, plus mountain biking in Whistler were possible options.

As expected, the scenery driving from Vancouver to Whistler was spectacular. Turquoise, glacier-fed lakes were nestled between soaring, snow-topped mountains. The air was snapping fresh and the people so gosh darn nice. We developed a major crush on Canada.

In Whistler, the mountain biking was intimidating. A whole ski hill of moguls, jumps, and trails was turned into a mountain biking mecca. Impossibly fit and ripped twentysomethings careened down the hills, completed jumps, and strutted about the plaza at the base of the mountain. We were agog. But when I saw some dads and a few women in their thirties and forties also doing it, I figured this formerly fit, occasional gym-visiting momma could manage it. Oh, the misguided thinking of middle age.

Thankfully, my son, Jack, and I snagged a female instructor who was older than 20, patient, and encouraging. After scrambling to heft our bikes on the chairlift, we began our class up on top of the mountain—which obviously left no escape hatch. We were committed. Young son picked up the maneuvers immediately: riding up banked hills and shifting body weight, staying crouched and *off the seat* the whole time, and generally riding the bike like he was auditioning for an X-games commercial. I took a little more time to master the moves. It was riding like I never had before. (Did I mention you can *never* sit down? Or that your legs shake and quiver with the isometric strain of staying in a crouched position while clutching the handlebars in a death grip?) It was totally foreign but fun.

Then we were off. We careened down that hill, banking the turns and rattling through sections like a bear was chasing us. (And on Jack's second run, he did see a bear.) I wiped out once but was pretty much unharmed aside from some road rash. When our instructor offered a second tour down, I demurred. But Jack joined her.

So later that day when we decided to take a leisurely family bike ride around a lake on a flat trail, I wasn't cautious. I should have been. On an extremely gentle slope, while going relatively slow, the gravel shifted under me, and I wiped out so hard on my side that I thought I was going to puke from the pain. I had fractured my arm years before, and this hurt just as bad. But worst of all, I was scheduled to go ziplining the next day!

In the emergency room, I asked if this was feasible. They rolled their eyes and said, "We've seen crazier. There are plenty of young skiers that get back on the slopes despite our cautionary advice." That's all I needed to hear. I was *not* canceling. With my arm in a sling and lots of ice and Ibuprofen, I headed back to our hotel.

"Your arm is in a *sling*!" admonished my husband, "What if you injure it further?"

"Mom, I think you're being crazy," said my son. But I was unde-terred. The X-rays showed it wasn't broken or fractured. And I might not ever make it back here again. I wanted to zipline.

The next day I took extra Ibuprofen and headed down to the regis-tration desk. I had slipped off my sling and tucked it inside my wind-breaker. *No need to advertise my condition,* I thought. After signing some waivers that promised I wouldn't sue if I became unhinged—literally—and including but not excluding dismemberment and plastering my panties, I was good to go.

We gathered at the rendezvous spot, where I was surrounded by fit and frenetic twentysomethings, plus one mom and her eight-year-old daughter. I quickly sized up the people around me. As women do when entering a room full of people (or at least, I have known some that do this—not that I have any firsthand experience), I scanned the group to see if I was the heaviest. For once, this was not a vanity issue. For me, it was a safety issue. If there was a heavier person who went before I did, and they came out unscathed, I figured I was pretty safe. I may be adventurous, but I'm not stupid.

A couple of men from Toronto joined our little group, and my heart lifted. They were about 6 feet 2 inches tall, solidly built, and easily outweighed me by 40 pounds. Yay! I was not destined to die. At least not today.

We got fitted with helmets and ropes and harnesses. The fitting of the harnesses was reminiscent of an airport pat down. The gear snuggles against your groin and hooks on to your ropes and stuff connected to your chest. You get briefly touched in places that you'd rather not. But for the sake of a secure fit? Have at it. There was a heck of a lot more ropes and metal clips and carabiners than I was aware we would need. Plus, we were supposed to lug the extra ropes and fas-teners on our shoulders from station to station along our trail route.

"Trails? Route?" I asked, "What do you mean?" I thought we

would be mainly sailing along the treetops, not pretending to be Sherpas and hauling a bunch of equipment around. (Did I mention my arm was throbbing and killing me?) I started to wonder if this was such a bright idea. How was I going to manage carrying these ropes and waddle around in my new thong harness? (Which was now bunching up my pants like an uncomfortable diaper.) But before I could thoroughly weigh these issues, we were hustled into a lift and started up the mountain.

After reaching the top of the mountain, we walked, waddled, and clattered a short distance to our first platform. The view was stunning. Impossibly pristine Canadian wilderness towered around us. A ginormous, gorgeous chasm yawned before us. And the postage stamp platform lay in front of us.

We crowded around the platform while our guides did fancy finagling with the ropes, clips, and machinations of the zipline apparatus. As I looked out over the vast, old growth forests, I thought the ziplines looked like gossamer threads. Merely cobwebs, dancing between the two gaping stations. Not something I wanted to be dangling from at 600 feet in the air and 50 miles an hour.

"So," I asked one of the workers, trying to maintain a jovial air, "has anyone ever fallen off one of these things?" This baby-man, who didn't look like he was shaving yet, looked up from his work and laughed. "Not yet!" Ha ha. I adjusted my throbbing arm and swallowed. I wished I had water. No, then I would have to pee. I wished I could vomit discreetly somewhere. Everyone else was squealing at the view and chattering nervously. Good. At least they were as jittery as I was. My teeth were starting to buzz as they do when I'm nervous, and my palms began to get clammy with sweat. I took deep breaths and tried to focus on the crisp, clean air I was inhaling. The magnificent view. This wonderful opportunity. The fact that baby-man said no one had died... *Yet.*

One of the instructors gathered us closer. "Now don't freak out, but sometimes people can get stuck." *Stuck?* This is a fine time to tell us. After they have my money and I'm stranded up on this mountain. He went on, "It happens if you're too light," they looked at the girl, "or too heavy."

I raised my hand, "You mean, you are just out there, dangling from that wire? Not moving?" *Yes.*

Apparently this is "not a big deal" because they can come out to you on the parallel wire and drag you back in. Super! Their advice to our girl was to draw her legs up to her chest and make her body a "ball," thereby reducing the wind resistance and upping the chance she would cruise all the way across. They didn't think any of us would have "too heavy" issues.

Finally, the moment had come. Somebody had to go first. We all looked at each other bug-eyed, as if we were facing the guillotine, when the mom spoke up. "My niece and I will go first!" Huh. So it wasn't her daughter after all. The young lady was her *niece*, an easy sacrifice.

They stood side by side on the edge of the platform, hundreds of feet in the air to prepare for a tandem ride as the workers hooked them up to the cobwebs overhead. There was a lot of joking and commenting, but eventually, that moment arrives. That crystalline moment where fighter pilots, stage actors, and surgeons have to take a deep breath and say, "Let's do this." The metal safety gates clanged open, and they screamed in unison as they stepped out into nothing but air. They dipped down gently and then whooshed out over the evergreen canopy, their pulleys making a metallic *bzzzzzzz* sound as they whizzed along the wires. We had barely started whooping and hollering for them when they became specs in the distance in a matter of seconds. We could hardly see them arriving at the next landing. But apparently they made it safe and sound because the walkie-talkie on baby-man squawked, "Next!"

After them went one of the burly guys—screaming like a girl and laughing maniacally. That eased my worries. Not that he was obviously more mentally unstable than I, but that he was the heaviest in the group. If the equipment was going to fail, it would be with him. It held fast.

Gate dude pointed at me. "You next?" And my dry mouth fell open without words. Burly man's friends patted me on the back, "Sure! She's next!" They roared with laughter and nudged me forward.

Standing behind that gate as I prepared to step into nothingness, trusting in my equipment, reminded me of that scene in the third *Raiders of the Lost Ark* movie where Indiana Jones has to step off of a cliff edge into thin air. He is promised in his guidebook that this "leap of faith" will work out okay. A deep chasm plunges before him. But before he steps out, he's a sweating, nervous wreck. The moment he commits his weight to that step and leans into it, the path appears and solidifies under his feet.

I thought about all the other times I stepped out, trusting I would be caught. Moving to Australia for a new job, wondering if I would hate it, be stuck for a year, and miss everyone back home too much. Stepping down the aisle with my husband and trusting our love and commitment would be enough to hold our marriage. But the most significant was in college when, realizing I had a lot of religion growing up but not much of a relationship with Jesus, I asked Him to come into my heart. It felt identical to stepping into the great, unknown void.

> The moment he commits his weight to that
> step and leans into it, the path appears
> and solidifies under his feet.

I knew I didn't want to go to Africa and get all sweaty and hot in missionary work. I knew that this decision wasn't a guarantee of an easy life. If anything, I felt like I would have a target on my back.

Lovely people, missionaries, and Christians die every day, even as they are serving others. But the promises were just too tantalizing to turn away from. In the book of John, Jesus promised, "I came that they may have life, and have it abundantly" (John 10:10 NASB). That was something better than the empty promises of more partying with my sorority. He also promised me forgiveness from all my shameful things. "If we confess our sins, He is faithful and righteous to forgive us our sins and to cleanse us from all unrighteousness" (1 John 1:9 NASB). I took note of that word *all*. That sounded like sweet relief.

Although my soul was in a sling, and I had my reservations about whether it would all work out, I offered up a lame prayer. It was full of doubt, confusion, and a whole lot of hope, that this thread of belief would catch and hold me. So I stepped into what felt like nothing but air. And discovered it was really the surety of eternity.

Those memories fluttered through my mind as I prepared to venture into yet another great unknown. So, like Indy, I stepped out into the void.

Like the others, I dipped down and for a split second thought, "Oh man! I would be the one it would fail on." But then I bounced up and began whizzing through the sky. Hundreds of feet below me were the tips of evergreens, whirling around me were the majestic mountains of Canada.

But it was all zipping past me in a blur. I had a death grip on my harness, as if I was solely responsible for keeping myself aloft in this spinning vortex. I could dimly hear the yells of the others, but my eyes were transfixed on the apparatus above me. Would it hold? How exactly was it working? Never mind the gorgeous scenery. I couldn't tear my gaze from what was holding me up. Thus, I was unprepared for the braking moment. I went from 50 to 5 miles an hour in a shuddering bounce, smashing my arm against the harness. I slowly cruised onto the arrival platform, and my group cheered me on.

"Wasn't that fantastic?" they yelled. "Wasn't that just amazing scenery?"

I didn't know what to answer. Because, truth was, I was so busy fixating on the apparatus holding me up, I didn't get to see much of the view. My eyes were glued to all the things I had no control over, and I missed out on much of it.

This happens a lot in life. I fuss and fret over things which I have absolutely no control over, and I miss out on the glorious journey. Life is throbbing and pulsating with wonder all around me, and the magical moments whiz by because I am focused on the wrong things.

My husband and I spent months arguing over sleep issues with our son when he was an infant. Instead of enjoying the time we had to spend rocking him (and remembering that the Kehler family tree has a long line of legendary insomniacs), I wasted time blaming Tom. Yelling at him. Crying a lot while Jack cried. Blaming the sleep books and their "experts." We could have just shrugged our shoulders and said, "Oh well, he's obviously a Kehler," and carried on with our lives.

Eventually, I realized that it wasn't the end of the world if he had to be rocked to sleep. It meant I could pray lengthy prayers over him to bless his life. I wish I had just embraced it sooner instead of obsessing over "the right way" to do sleep and raging at the world.

We can't "fix" our spouses or our children or much of life. But we can choose to fix our eyes on what matters. "Jesus loves me! This I know, for the Bible tells me so," say the lyrics to the song every Sunday school kid learns. It's pretty simple. God's got this. He loves you. He can hold you. All your worries, doubts and failures, and fixations, He's got this. Enjoy the ride.

> God's got this. He can hold you. All your worries,
> doubts and failures, and fixations,
> He's got this. Enjoy the ride.

On the next leg of our journey, I determined I would let go and let the ride sweep me along. As before, we had to step off the platform into the insubstantial. The sweet, clean air whistled past as I gazed in wonderment at the beauty before me. I gave no more thought to what was holding me up and just reveled in the sensation of flying. It was even better than what the brochure promised.

And despite having to hike around the woods from platform to platform, and schlepping our gear, it was one glorious ride after another. I never got tired of the views of all four runs, or the sensation of soaring. In fact, on our fourth zipline run, I turned upside down like our leaders instructed us to do for a really awesome perspective. The lesson of that day is indelibly stamped on my memory.

God's got this. When I let go of my illusion of control, I can really enjoy the ride.

Exploring Further

1. Have you ever foolishly rushed into something without thinking twice?
2. What claims of Jesus or Bible passages most draw your heart toward Him?
3. In what areas of your life are you trying to control things as opposed to trusting God?

21

Sunsets

Deep plum, slate gray, and indigo cloud mountains bruised the sky. They towered overhead like an impending storm. Underneath, at the ocean's horizon, a thin line of salmon pink merged into an impossible fire of fuchsia and electric orange. The soft sounds of car doors thumping closed came from behind us. The lot was filling up. Quietly, the worshippers crunched through the gravel to stand beside us at the cliff's edge. A biting wintry gust ruffled our hair, and we hunched our shoulders, tucked our chins down into our scarves, determined to wait it out.

The hushed voices around us were reverently commenting on the riotous palette developing before us. The elderly, the surfers—still damp from their session—the bikers, and the parents stood shoulder to shoulder in mutual adoration. Then the blazing fireball peeked below the cloud curtain, and we were blinded. Brilliant light washed over us; we squinted against the intensity. As it sank below the horizon, we stood mesmerized, bathed in a warm pumpkin glow of reflection. Finally, it dipped completely out of sight and, one by one, the devotees turned and headed back to their warm homes.

Despite the wintry time of year, we had all decided to put down the tools of our trades and intentionally pay homage to this heliocentric moment of awe. But it made me wonder—why is it that winter sunsets are often so much more dramatic and colorful than those in the summer?

I first noticed this growing up in Wisconsin. Summer sunsets were tranquil and lovely. But in the winter, when the thermometer often hovered below zero—even by 20 degrees—the colors of our midwestern sky were splashed with psychedelic fire. Impossible magenta, violet, and neon pinks streaked across the sky. It seemed incongruous to have such a riot of color over the frozen and whitened landscape. It wasn't unusual to hear my mother exclaim, "Come quick! Look what God is painting across the sky tonight!"

According to the National Oceanic and Atmospheric Administration, sunset colors are based on how light moves through the atmosphere. Pollution, pollen, and dust particles in the air scatter light and lessen the amount that travels to the ground, and so reduces the sunset's vibrancy. Therefore, when you have a hazy day, colors in the sunset will be more subdued. On a clear day, the hours around dusk produce more vibrant and intense colors. NOAA states:

> Because air circulation is more sluggish during the summer, and because the photochemical reactions which result in the formation of smog and haze proceed most rapidly at that time of the year, late fall and winter are the most favored times for sunrise and sunset viewing over most of the United States.[1]

So even though it was winter in our little town along the coast, the spectacular display drew us strangers out of the warmth of our homes and cars into a congenial congregation united in devotion.

Sunsets are the communal table of nature. Their splendor summons us to a collective experience of transcendence and awe. All are welcome. All have an equal seat. And so every culture and person ceases striving and pauses for a glorious sunset blazing across the sky.

Sunsets are the communal table of nature. Their splendor summons us to a collective experience of transcendence and awe. All are welcome.

I've shared magnificent sunsets across deserts, in the mountains, in Hawaii, Micronesia, and Norway. And the behavior of the awed viewers everywhere is the same. We stop, we talk in hushed tones, even to strangers, and we appreciate that something massive and magnificent, something transcendent—beyond our control—is happening before us. Shared beauty makes friends of strangers. We don't ask each other if we are Republican, Democrat, Christian, atheist, or Hindu. We stand shoulder to shoulder in admiration, thankful for the moment and of one belief: This moment is worthy of our attention. This is worthy of our admiration.

Oftentimes there is a more glorious show that most people miss. They leave right after the sun disappears, believing that the sunset is "over." I feel sad for them because it is most definitely not over. There is more to come. Some of the most outrageous colors and cloud formations occur minutes and half hours after the sun has departed. The afterglow, the remnants, can be even more startling. The colors deepen, from fire-hot oranges to deep corals and crimsons. Indigos and mauves transition to dark eggplant purple and navy blues. They shift, change, and intensify their dance of drama in the absence of the sun. The aftermath, the remains, can be the most beautiful part of the show.

I saw this in my mother's life after she died. I knew that she had taught blind children how to swim. I knew that she had volunteered for various charitable services, and I knew that she had friends who adored her. But I saw it more fully in the aftermath of her life, after she had departed from the scene. After my mother was gone, the colors of her influence spread even further.

One by one, people talked about how giving she was. They mentioned her exuberance, her laughter, her kindness and thoughtfulness. We reminisced about her bringing casseroles to new neighbors, delivering meals to shut-ins, and organizing a team of needlepoint stitchers to make kneelers for communion at church. She wasn't a powerful executive, and she didn't bring in an income, but her influence on the community was huge.

> After my mother was gone, the colors of
> her influence spread even further.

Through eulogies, testimonies, obituaries, and letters, the impact of her heart of service and buoyant attitude carried on. Her friends kept coming up to our family and sharing wonderful stories about her servant heart.

She's not the only one whose influence lingers long after her sun has set.

We still sing John Newton's song "Amazing Grace" more than 200 years after he left this earth. And for the enquiring mind, his background story of slave-trading, whoring, and living to the lowest depths of depravity are instructive. For in this song, long after his sunset, millions learn about how it doesn't matter if you've been a "wretch." That the love of God can transform any life, no matter how dark and hellish. That we all can experience "how wide and long and high and deep is the love of Christ, and to know this love that surpasses knowledge—that you may be filled to the measure of all the fullness of God" (Ephesians 3:18-19). What remains long after Newton's colorful life is a glorious testimony of rescue and deliverance.

Most of the time, people don't think about what legacy they are going to leave behind until they get up in years. Then they do some interesting things. Some like to throw their names onto buildings. And I always wonder, will people 50 years later know who they are or what they stood for? Or will they assume, like I do, that someone with a large ego wanted to be remembered, so they chiseled their name on this building? But I have no idea who they were or what they stood for.

If they don't name a building after themselves, they might decide they want to be buried in their car or leave their money for their pets. All noteworthy and interesting. But eternal significance? No.

We can learn much from those who have no more time left. Their suns are setting, and they wished they would have lived life differently. I found this list put together by palliative care nurse Bronnie Ware, who gathered it based on her discussions with her dying patients. She took care of them for the last three to twelve weeks of their lives. Her patients talked about their lives, what they wish they had done, and what they had left undone. This list is heartbreaking.[2]

1. I wish I'd had the courage to live a life true to myself, not the life others expected of me.

This was the most common theme, living someone else's dreams or desires for us. Whether it's our parents, friends, or spouses, we need to live *our* lives, not the life they want us to live.

2. I wish I hadn't worked so hard.

Almost every single male Bronnie helped expressed this lament. They missed out on raising their children and the companionship of their partner's youth. Since her clients were of an older generation, she suspects that women—who are working more now than earlier generations—will be saying this as well.

3. I wish I'd had the courage to express my feelings.

Bronnie writes, "Many people suppressed their feelings in order to keep peace with others. As a result, they settled for a mediocre existence and never became who they were truly capable of becoming. Many developed illnesses relating to the bitterness and resentment they carried as a result."

4. I wish I had stayed in touch with my friends.

Most of us think about getting our finances in order, but these people realized that money and status mean nothing. In the end, it was all about love and relationships. For many, it was too late to track down a long-lost friend they hadn't kept in touch with.

5. I wish that I had let myself be happier.

This was more common than you would expect. Most people never realized that happiness is a choice. Don't let that slip by: *Happiness is a choice.* It is not dependent on what people think of you or what's been done to you. You can still choose your attitude. Remember the adage, "Most folks are about as happy as they make up their minds to be." Nazi Holocaust survivor and psychiatrist Viktor Frankl echoed this thought. Despite his suffering in the concentration camps, he opined, "Everything can be taken from a man but one thing: the last of the human freedoms—to choose one's attitude in any given set of circumstances, to choose one's own way."[3]

Too late did these dying people realize how little it mattered what others thought of them. They wished they had lived with more laughter, silliness, and delight. Instead, they convinced themselves they were fine and let mediocrity and comfort rule.

Instead of a palette of blazing colors, unforgettable moments, and lives lived to the fullest, Ware's patients were leaving behind lives of beige. Nothing ventured, nothing risked, and no legacy to inspire others long after they are gone.

So how can we live so we leave behind that is worth admiring? What kind of life choices can we make so that others gaze at the remnants and sigh, "Wow, that's gorgeous"? In what I've observed, we can leave behind a glorious palette when we give instead of grasp, bow instead of brag, and seek a purpose instead of a platform.

Contrary to what social media lead us to believe, the notable people who are universally admired don't chase happiness, or fame, or money. They don't concern themselves with what other people think about them. They don't run and search for the ultimate spouse, experience, or lifestyle. Instead of grasping, they give. Instead of bragging, they bow to serve others. Instead of seeking a platform, they seek a purpose. They pour themselves out for others. They serve. They serve by using their talents of leadership, hospitality, administration, teaching, technology, or wherever their sweet spot of joy and the world's needs meet.

We can leave behind a glorious palette when we give instead of grasp, bow instead of brag, and seek a purpose instead of a platform.

This is not sexy or glamorous, but it is eternal. It is joyful. Those who touch lives in daycares, soup kitchens, hospitals, offices, schools, jails, and our neighborhood coffee shops have joy on their faces. They are the kind of people I want to hang out with. They choose the palette of activities that leave behind a beautiful work of art.

I hope that we can all say like the apostle Paul,

> For I am already being poured out like a drink offering, and the time for my departure is near. I have fought the good fight, I have finished the race, I have kept the faith. Now there is in store for me the crown of righteousness, which the Lord, the righteous Judge, will award to me on that day—and not only to me, but also to all who have longed for his appearing (2 Timothy 4:6-8).

Although Paul was fading from the scene, he was confident he was leaving behind a glorious work of art, pleasing to his heavenly Father. We can do the same. Let's pick up our palettes.

Exploring Further

1. What are some of the most memorable sunsets you have seen? Who were you with?
2. Which item(s) in that list by the palliative care nurse really spoke to you?
3. Do you think the world has a different view of a life well lived than what the Bible says? Why or why not?
4. What are you doing in your life now to leave a lasting legacy? How has this journey inspired you to do something differently?

Notes

Why Nature Matters

1. Richard Louv, *Last Child in the Woods* (New York: Workman Publishing, 2008), 32.
2. Rachel McCormick, "Does Access to Green Space Impact the Mental Well-being of Children?" *Journal of Pediatric Nursing,* http://www.pediatricnursing.org/article/S0882-5963(17)30185-9/abstract, accessed April 3, 2018.
3. Nadia Drake, "Beyond the Blue Marble," *National Geographic,* March 2018.
4. Ibid.

Chapter 5: Wind

1. Colin Melbourne, "Scottish Hebrides Revival of 1949," The Faith Mission, www.born-again-christian.info/scottish.hebrides.revival.duncan.campbell.htm, accessed March 11, 2018.

Chapter 6: Compass

1. "Geomagnetism Frequently Asked Questions," National Oceanic and Atmospheric Administration, https://www.ngdc.noaa.gov/geomag/faqgeom.shtml#What_happens_to_my_compass_in_the_southern_hemisphere, accessed April 3, 2018.

Chapter 7: Falconry

1. Sarah Zylstra, "Died: Robert McQuilkin, College President Praised for Alzheimer's Resignation," *Christianity Today,* http://www.christianitytoday.com/news/2016/june/died-robertson-mcquilkin-columbia-president-alzheimers-ciu.html.
2. Ibid.
3. Jamie Ivey, *If You Only Knew* (Nashville, TN: B&H Publishing Group, 2018), 118-19.

Chapter 9: Campfire

1. Johann Hari (February 2013). Johann Hari: Everything You Think You Know About Addiction Is Wrong [video file], https://www.ted.com/talks/johann_hari_everything_you_think_you_know_about_addiction_is_wrong.
2. Johann Hari, *Lost Connections* (New York: Bloomsbury, 2018), 99.
3. John Ortberg, *Everybody's Normal Till You Get to Know Them* (Grand Rapids, MI: Zondervan: Willow Creek Resources, 2003), 32.

Chapter 10: Survival

1. Elisabeth Elliot, *Secure in the Everlasting Arms* (Ann Arbor, MI: Servant Publications, 2002), 50.

2. Louis Zamperini, *Don't Give Up, Don't Give In* (New York: Dey Street Books, 2014), 71-72.

Chapter 12: Stars

1. John Muir, *Travels in Alaska* (publishing info 1915), 5.

Chapter 14: Fireflies

1. Gregory Boyle, *Tattoos on the Heart* (New York: Free Press, 2010), 9.

2. Homeboy Industries, https://www.homeboyfoods.com/aboutus.asp.

3. Madeleine L'Engle, *Walking on Water* (Wheaton, IL: Shaw Publishers, 1980), 122.

Chapter 16: Startfish

1. Peter Crutchley, "Did a Prayer Meeting Really Bring Down the Berlin Wall and End the Cold War?" http://www.bbc.co.uk/religion/0/24661333, accessed April 13, 2018.

Chapter 17: Monarch

1. https://www.edf.org/ecosystems/monarch-butterfly-habitat-exchange

2. http://www.gems-girls.org/about/mission-history

3. https://www.a21.org/

Chapter 19: Mountain Lion

1. http://mountainlion.org/FAQfrequentlyaskedquestions.asp.

2. C.S. Lewis *The Screwtape Letters* (New York: HarperOne, 1996), 32.

3. Based on verses 1 John 3:8; Revelation 1:18; John 4:4; Philippians 2:10-11.

Chapter 21: Sunsets

1. Stephen F. Corfidi, "The Colors of Sunset and Twilight," NOAA/NWS Storm Prediction Center, www.spc.noaa.gov/publications/corfidi/sunset/, accessed August, 29 2017.

2. Bronnie Ware, "Regrets of the Dying," www.bronnieware.com/blog/regrets-of-the-dying, accessed August 29, 2017.

3. Viktor Frankl, *Man's Search for Meaning* (Boston, MA: Beacon Press, 2006), 66.

Acknowledgments

A heartfelt thanks to you, reader! You took your precious time to go on this adventure with me. I am deeply grateful. Please leave a review on Amazon! It makes a difference.

I thank my agent, the terrific Tawny Johnson for her passion and belief in this project. You are a delight to work with and a gas to laugh with.

I'm tickled and grateful for the zeal Harvest House exhibited over this book. Your enthusiasm and excitement humbled me and spurred me to deliver more than what you expected. In this world of publishing behemoths, you are a treasure—stealthy, smart, and steadfast.

I'm indebted to my critique group: Pat J. Sikora, Gabriela Banks, Stephanie Shoquist, and Christie Naler. Thank you all for your editorial contributions, laughter, and prayers.

Thank you to my beta readers: Lynne Hurrell, Laura Yannazzo, Lori Holmlund, Darby Moyer, Emma Lodge, Jessica Read, Amanda Andrus, Kelly Shank, Heather Fignar, Kate Radcliffe, Denise Sultenfuss, Judith Grace, Lynne Hartke, Natalie Ogbourne, Noreen Sevret, Lindsey Hartz. Your feedback was invaluable!

More Books by Laurie Kehler

Gardening Mercies—Finding God in Your Garden

Wings of Mercy—Spiritual Reflections from the Birds of the Air

For more free resources, please visit:
www.ThisOutsideLife.com/bookresources

To learn more about Harvest House books and
to read sample chapters, visit our website:

www.harvesthousepublishers.com

HARVEST HOUSE PUBLISHERS
EUGENE, OREGON
